THE COUNTRYMAN'S YESTERDAY

Thorp Arch village, near Tadcaster, Yorkshire. (John Edenbrow)

THE COUNTRYMAN'S YESTERDAY

Edited by
Christopher Hall

PELHAM BOOKS/Stephen Greene Press

PELHAM BOOKS/Stephen Greene Press

Published by the Penguin Group
27 Wrights Lane, London W8 5TZ, England
Viking Penguin Inc., 40 West 23rd Street, New York, New York 10010, USA
The Stephen Greene Press, Inc., 15 Muzzey Street, Lexington, Massachusetts 02173, USA

Penguin Books Australia Ltd, Ringwood, Victoria, Australia
Penguin Books Canada Ltd, 2801 John Street, Markham, Ontario, Canada L3R 1B4
Penguin Books (NZ) Ltd, 182–190 Wairau Road, Auckland 10, New Zealand

Penguin Books Ltd, Registered Offices: Harmondsworth, Middlesex, England

First published 1989

Copyright © The Countryman 1989

Typeset by Cambridge Photosetting Services

Made and printed in Great Britain by Butler & Tanner Ltd, Frome, Somerset

A CIP catalogue record for this book is available from the British Library.

ISBN 0 7207 1902 X

CONTENTS

Christopher Hall, Editor of The Countryman. (Fay Godwin)

FOREWORD

For more than sixty years, *Country-man* readers have dipped into each issue of the little green magazine as it arrives. It is not a journal to read through from cover to cover. Successive editors have constructed it with the idea that each new issue should be a rural brantub in which the reader can browse and discover for himself or herself, by chance as well as by design.

This anthology of goodies from past brantubs has been put together on the same principle. I took back numbers off the shelf and browsed until something caught my interest or fancy. Then I dipped in and – usually – I pulled out a plum.

The thread is that all the pieces of writing offered here look back. We have called the collection *The Countryman's Yesterday,* but some pieces go back to the day before yesterday, and perhaps even the day before that. Some were written by people recreating the past; some by people remembering their own. And some are pieces which were about contemporary scenes when written, but the scenes have now passed into yesterday.

There is much here which is nostalgic for the past. But some of the pieces remind us of harsher realities. On *The Countryman,* while we rejoice in the British countryside, we never forget that J. W. Robertson Scott founded the magazine in the 1920s – a time of deep rural depression – to crusade against insanitary homes, rotten schools, starvation wages, incompetent farmers and greedy landowners. He knew that to win people of all classes and parties to support the 'rural advance', which he sought to promote, he must entertain and intrigue as well as persuade them. That is what we have been doing ever since.

But when all is said, the aim of this collection is to remind you of the riches and variety of the countryside. Of Cornish pasties, Suffolk punches, Welsh hill-farmers, Hereford hops, sheep on the Cumbrian fells, village buses in the Cotswolds, green roads in the Yorkshire Dales, village chapels in east Yorkshire – and much else.

We have thrown into the tub a liberal sprinkling too of the 'fillers' for which the magazine is famous: scraps of poetry, anecdotes in dialect and the pithy, salty sayings gleaned from countryfolk which make up our long-running 'Tail Corn' column.

I met a lot of old friends and made a lot of new ones in the process of putting the collection together. I hope you'll do the same as you dip in.

Christopher Hall
Editor of The Countryman

COUNTRY CHILDHOODS

THE NIGHT OF THE WELL
Hilary Higgins

The sudden cold air bit ferociously into my throat and the uneven bricks, glazed with frost, slid treacherously beneath my feet. Behind me, the half-open door spilled a beam of yellow light down the double step. In front, the icy darkness – and the well.

I was twelve, and about to draw water for the first time. The pails clinked in my hands as I shook with cold and terror. Even in broad daylight the deep black pit held who-knew-what horrors. Now this was the lonely night with only the stars and a finger-nail moon to pierce the blackness.

We were still in transition then – no longer Londoners, but not yet at one with the rurality to which we had come six months ago. Mushrooms in the fields and a tame pheasant begging at the door enchanted us. Not being able to command gallons of hot and cold water, at the turn of a tap, did not.

Our new next-door neighbour had shown us how to operate the well. The wooden roller had slipped between his brown hands, smoothly lowering the bucket-laden chain into the depths. We heard the distant splash as water was reached and watched the dextrous rewinding.

'This'll do you till tea-time,' he told us, pouring the shining treasure into our waiting pails.

It did not. It barely stretched from breakfast to elevenses. When he'd drawn us four loads, with tea-time still a remote landmark, my mother declared she must tackle the job herself. I promptly shepherded the younger ones out into the garden to keep them away from the yawning hole which dominated the enclosed brick yard between the cottages and their outhouses.

It wasn't long before my elder sister – a grown-up fourteen – learnt to draw her own water for her constant ablutions, but I, content with lesser attentions, did not have this spur and managed to avoid the well by performing other, less hazardous tasks. The very sight of that inky hole filled me with terror.

'That's a proper bit of work,' our neighbour once told me. 'Look at the way them bricks fits all round neat. And no cement neither 'cept for the top few courses.' I recalled building sites in London. 'You have to have cement,' I told him. 'I've seen builders bricklaying.'

He gave a derisive snort. 'House-builders! Them as made this 'ere well were *well*-builders. That's all they did, build wells, and all by hand. No machines. Look!' He crossed to the well and lifted the wooden hatch. 'You look 'ere.'

My stomach plunging, I nervously approached. His weathered finger pointed. 'You see those missed-out bits. Those are left out a-purpose so Old Perce, he can put in the putlocks and climb out. Old Ben, 'e's up the top 'ere carting the spoil away and Old Perce 'e's down there digging.' Someone down there! My spine crawled. To my relief, he closed the hatch.

He drew a tin from his pocket and began rolling a very small cigarette. 'I mind them telling me about this 'ere well. Took days and days to dig. Old Perce, he were beginning to wonder if he'd been told the wrong place to dig, but then one morning Old Ben, he hears a shout and come and looked down – and Old Perce, he looks up and says, "Got any dry boots up there because there ain't none down 'ere." Just like that.' He shook with a sudden chuckle. 'And then Perce, he starts bricking fast as he can go, 'cause once that water starts, it keeps coming and he has to dig down under it so much to give a bit of bucket room as he calls it.' He shook his head, remembering. 'Weren't nobody to replace them when they went. Ah well . . . ' and still shaking his head, he stumped off to his cabbages.

Comforting though it was to know our drinking water came from a properly constructed source, I still wanted none of its fetching and always managed to be elsewhere when a drawer was required. So skilfully did I achieve this that no one had any inkling of my secret fear. But it couldn't last. That icy night, my mother was getting the youngest two washed for bed by the fire while my younger sister and I tackled a jigsaw puzzle. Father was out and my elder sister was setting her newly-washed hair on a complicated conglomeration of pink and blue plastic rollers.

'Put some water on quickly for their hot-water bottles,' my mother asked me. 'I've forgotten to do them.'

Not thinking, I went at once to the kitchen where the water pails stood in the corner. Both were empty. I stood there as the full realisation of my dilemma settled appallingly.

'There's no water left,' I reported. My mother, busily holding pyjamas out to warm in the heat from the fire, barely glanced round. 'Go and draw some then, would you?' My eldest sister continued winding rollers unconcernedly. The die was cast. I picked up the pails and went out. Why, oh why hadn't I served my apprenticeship in the long, bright summer hours? Why had I saved it for this cold, dark night?

The iron ring on the well cover was so cold it seemed to burn my fingers. Perhaps I should fetch my gloves? But I knew that once I looked back I should never muster courage to plough this particular furrow again. I picked up the shiny galvanised bucket and held it over the well-mouth while I wound the handle to take up the slack chain. Gripping the handle now with both hands, I began to lower the bucket into the void. Link by link the chain paid out, until at last I heard the faint splash of metal on water and the chain slackened. Slowly now the other way to bring the load up. My confidence grew and I began to wind with more speed. Soon the bucket appeared and I reached out – only to draw back in dismay. It was almost empty. I hadn't let it down far enough to fill.

With a sigh I began again. My fingers were almost numb with cold and my feet in their thin shoes rapidly joining in. I longed to be back in the warm. This time I wound more confidently and I was soon drawing up a far heavier haul. Half-way up it began to swing and I did not know how to stop it. Soon it was bouncing off the bricks sending jars right through the ground below my feet.

At last it was at the top. I reached over to swing the bucket towards me in the approved manner. But alas, my untrained arms were no match for two heavy gallons of water. It tipped and spilled in an icy tidal wave over my shoes. I nearly wept with frustration and cold.

However, half a bucket was ample for

'It tipped and spilled in an icy tidal wave . . .' (Anne Roper)

hot-water bottles and bedtime drinks, so I decanted my remaining water into the waiting pails. I closed the hatch with a shudder of relief and then hurried indoors with a glorious sense of mission accomplished. It wasn't until I was about to fill the kettle that I noticed a perfect blizzard of black moss fragments in each pail, gathered from the brick lining as the bucket bumped upwards.

But my apprenticeship had been served. In the years that followed, I went to the well many times a week. Never, admittedly, without a shudder for the deep pit and an aversion of the eyes from Perce's footholds. But I went, and eventually became as proficient as our neighbour in drawing full shining loads with never a drop spilt.

We children grew up, married and now have homes of our own. My parents and our old neighbour continue to live in their adjoining cottages. But five years ago the wooden hatch was closed for the last time. Piped water had been installed complete with scale, chlorination and regular bills. The old stone sinks were replaced by modern units, and above these gleam new taps as bright and shining as a bucket once gleamed on a dark, frosty night more than twenty years ago.

(Winter 1985)

(John Saunders)

COUNTRY CHILDREN

Driving along country roads in the early morning,
I pass children at the lane-ends, at the cold stops,
like milk churns. How warm their kitchens must be
and awful to leave, to stamp grey light into warmth beneath the dripping trees.

I remember my city mornings: the close lit houses,
the sombre presence of adults and of a world
on its way to work; and come back to these –
the first or last children on the face of this earth:
their birthright, to stamp grey light to warmth beneath the dripping trees.

Tom Pow (Spring 1985)

THE KEY TO JOHNNY

Kathleen Gooding

When the school bell rang at four o' clock it was raining hard. 'Wait under the porch till it eases,' I told the children. Like swarming bees they hummed and buzzed obediently under its stone roof, looking at the driving storm, the country road and the flat green fields beyond: all except Johnny, a stocky brown-faced eight-year-old. He sprang straight into the downpour, slapping his hobnails into the puddles as though to wash off the very dust of school.

'You'll be soaked,' I said. 'Come back.' He turned, huddled against rain and authority: 'Granny said I got to get 'ome quick.' Then he raced round the churchyard wall and took the moor road home. I grabbed my mackintosh and ran after him.

The high-built road was a narrow white line between the flood-waters. Low dripping clouds hung down over the moor; arrow-heads bobbed in the racing rhines; long rows of half-submerged withies edged the fields. I could see Johnny, deaf to calls, scurrying along like a rabbit till he felt safe. Sometimes he stared up at the tall poplars or down into the brown water. He would be looking for woodpecker or owl holes, or the patterned black and white of a heron wading in a pool. Presently he turned out of sight up a narrow drove. At the far end, over a greenish plank that bridged the barton ditch, lay his grandmother's cottage and home.

Back in the grey stone two-teacher village school I looked at his books. His writing was smudged with effort, his simple primer blotched with tears and finger-prints. Earlier, as he sat in his usual numbed futility, I had taken a bird's feather to him: 'Which one is this, Johnny?' His face lit up; 'It be a golden plover's, I think, miss.'

'Do try,' I urged later. 'Let's learn these letters. Don't you want ever to read about Big Dog Tom?'

'No.'

The other children, all bright juniors, soared ahead. Johnny, wooden and apathetic, was alone. He could count: tallying turves and withy-spars with father had taught him that. In free expression his rhythmic movements were good, though limited – always the flap of a bird-wing or the swing of a sickle. But in reading and writing he stared hopeless and terrified at the meaningless symbols. How to break the reading block that fouled his progress, to reach that rich but fallow mind, bright with visions of kingfisher, robin, shapely geese-flight and roosting herons? Of all my pupils he mattered most.

I took my bicycle from the shed and set off in his wake. Beyond the moors stretched a long row of dark hills. Small spread clouds, like hedge-tufts of sheep's wool, blew before a rising wind. Floods rippled by the roadside or drooled over the sandbags; drowned grasses shifted in strange cathedral-like shapes beneath the surface. Johnny's cottage stood on a mound above the water. The air was fragrant with peat-smoke from the chimney, and there were rows of neatly built turf cones in the garden. In summer I rode out there to buy the snow-white celery his father grew in beds of black peat soil, or to carry back the huge cos lettuce which was the crispest in the world. On Saturdays I often met Johnny in villages miles away, his legs swinging over the tail-board of a turf-laden lorry, helping his father to sell from house to house.

I knocked at the door. It was opened by a bare-footed Johnny, who fell back as though visited by the wrath of God. 'I've only come to see if you arrived safely,' I lied. His granny was tossing turves on the fire, her brown face peering through a shower of red sparks and blue smoke. 'Sit down, miss. 'E were soaked through, boots an' all.' She pointed to the sodden objects hanging in the chimney. Then she gave me a cake from the pan which swung over the hearth, and a cup of hot peat-tasting tea. Johnny, sulky and wondering, lay on a rag rug by the fire, playing with a box of shells and pebbles. At the back of the cottage was the bedroom where he slept, lulled by the soft lapping of the rhine water beneath the sill. His father, who had just come in from sandbagging, also sat near the fire, eyeing me questioningly.

'I don't think 'e'll be in school tomorrow,' said Granny easily. 'Boots'll still be wet an' flood'll be worser.' Granny cared little for education.

''E will,' exclaimed Father unexpectedly. 'I c'n always row 'im. If that attendance officer comes 'ere again, it won't be thee what 'as to listen to 'is old pie-jaw. If Johnny don't go for nothin' else, then 'e c'n go to save me from that fellow.'

'Yes,' I said, undaunted, 'he shouldn't miss. His reading . . . '

'Don't 'e learn well?' demanded Father hotly.

'No,' I faltered.

'Don't 'e listen?'

'He listens, but . . . '

'Johnny!' he roared. 'Dussen't thee listen?' Johnny rose to his feet, nodding in terror. 'Do 'ee want to scrat for a livin' like I got to all thee days? Listen, boy, listen!'

Father, I felt, was a flood-water of a man whose dam was liable to break at any moment and sweep us all away. 'I thought perhaps a little gentle co-operation,' I began, 'some evening reading . . . '

'Belt it into 'un,' rumbled Father. 'I gives you leave. Punch 'is 'ead.'

'Reading!' snapped Granny from the opposition. 'The litter! I never read nothin' in me life an' I bain't the worser.' She clicked her needles angrily over a thick black stocking. Soon she would put a brick from the hot peats into Johnny's bed and mull him some cider as a nightcap against floods and educational worries. She was my best bet. 'He mustn't be frightened,' I said. 'No,' agreed Granny, glaring.

Emboldened by support, Johnny shyly brought me his box of eggs: 'Mallard, teal, moorhen, sandpiper, bunting . . . '

'You need some cotton-wool and a bit of glass. I'll get you some,' I told him, not wishing to discourage him then by asking where he had collected the eggs of so many protected birds.

I rode away, worried, in the silvery fading daylight. How wrong had I been? Homework was out; Father's misapplied vigour would ruin it. Then inspiration came. The bird book! It was in a trunk in my lodgings. It had been to me a disappointing present. Perhaps now it would be a joy to someone else. The titles were in simple capitals which even Johnny should find easy. There were coloured plates of birds, nests, eggs and habitats with simply written descriptions on the facing pages. It might be the key to his particular prison door.

'Wait behind a minute, Johnny,' I said after school the next day. I took out the roll of cotton-wool and gave him that first.

'Granny's give me some photo-frame glass,' he said joyfully.

'There's got to be some name-labels made,' I warned him, 'and you are going to make them. Have you got a pen at home?

No? Well, I'll lend you mine.' I took out the bird book. 'What bird is this?'

'A robin, miss.'

'Look underneath. See that word? What does it say?'

'R-O-B-I-N.'

Slowly we went through: lark, tit, finch, jay. He stood lost in delight, turning over pages, recognising birds and, with grubby tracing forefinger, finding the appropriate names. Beyond the window a funeral was taking place in the churchyard. This usually had a morbid fascination for Johnny; surreptitiously he would stand up in his seat when my back was turned, savouring it. Through the window I could see the red sunset, the white flowers, the small brown mound. Like the celandines on Plow Ridge after a sharp May frost, an old villager had faded away; and Johnny was not even looking.

'Martin, hawk, cuckoo, crane,' he read. 'Can I take the book 'ome to show Granny what I can do?'

'Take it home for keeps. And don't paddle in the flood-water. Granny said you got to go home quick.'

'Will you bring the pen tonight, miss?'

'Tonight,' I promised. Then I pushed the book under his arm and stood, watching his hobnails strike sparks out of the stones, as he took the moor road home.

(Autumn 1964)

BEES ARE PEOPLE

Ada Jackson

I was not allowed near the bees until my seventh year, and then only because Grandfather had his arm in a sling and could not cut the grass before the hives. Long grass, he told me, is death to the young bee; it is a forest to him, and he exhausts himself trying to find a way out. But before he left me with the kitchen scissors and a stretch of greensward, he introduced me to the hives. 'This is Mima's girl,' he said. 'She will not harm you. You can trust her.'

Several days and a few blisters later, I was filling the bees' shallow drinking pans with clean water and washed stones for them to alight on, and in no time at all I was as deeply involved as Grandfather with them. He talked by the hour of their wisdom, their industry, the perfection of their communal life, their selfless spirit. In times of small gatherings, he said, not one will take advantage of his fellows. If one should starve, they would all starve.

While we watched them he would interpret their various notes and ecstatic dances on the alighting board, and always spoke to them as if they were equals and could understand. Year by year we praised and thanked them for the honey yield and shared such news as the weight of the apple crop, the state of Aunt Hannah's poor knee, the joy of the new grandchild, my chances in the scholarship. They were happy days, but the happiest was when I tied white ribbons on the skeps and Aunt Jenny, rosy as an apple bough, came

through the door in her wedding dress. They said a bee went to church in her bouquet.

'Never fret yourself about the shape they wear,' Grandfather counselled me. 'Bees are people, and family, and have the right to be told what goes on.' And, he went on, if they were slighted or offended or kept out of things, they had their own ways of showing displeasure.

Childhood, people say, is the time when nobody dies. Something went from mine the day I saw Uncle Sam at the hives and heard him say, 'Bees, your master's dead. I am your master now.' With that he knocked on each hive, and from within came a stir and commotion. 'They know,' said my uncle, and we went indoors to find some strips of mourning for the hives.

When I went away to college, coming home only for holidays, I found the bees still thriving, the house smelling of bees-wax and the shelves full of honey. I would set out the bees' drinking water as before, cut the grass, and in a cold season feed cane syrup and pea flour as Grandfather had taught me; but the garden had become a smaller place, and I belonged to a wider world, stripped of fantasy. Nevertheless, when Uncle Sam died one Easter day, I went through the grey morning and rapped on the hives and gave the news, not entirely for old time's sake. I did not want the honey to be black.   *(Autumn 1967)*

ON EATING SLICED BREAD

What happened to the loaf of bread
That fed me as a boy?
Where has it gone, that buttered vice
That slice by every crusty slice
Brought rich and poor man joy?

The Miller Man now dead and gone
Would surely turn in pain,
If he could see now how they treat
The golden ear of his loved wheat
The King of all the grain.

And restless lies the Baker too
Besides the ones he fed.
So pale the Baker! Red the flame!
So sweet the bread that bore the name,
Now carved above his head.
                    Bob Bell (Summer 1986)

SNAKE IN THE GLASS

Joan Kent

My brother warned me of the snake inside our lamp. At night it was clearly visible coiled up in the translucent bowl and, when the lamp was filled, I could see it squirming like the viper we once found behind the water-butt.

The lamp had a base of twining iron vines and a multi-coloured globe that radiated light like sunshine through stained glass. It transformed our workaday farmhouse kitchen and was the axis of my childhood's winter world. I treated it with healthy respect, knowing that the snake waited like some evil genie in a bottle, ready to escape and eat whoever broke the lamp. The memory of that Saturday night when it was smashed is with me still.

My mother believed that if her children started each Sunday clean inside and out, nothing would ail them for the rest of the week. Each Saturday after tea the galvanised tin bath was placed on the flag-stoned scullery floor between the copper and the pump; and no matter how warm the water, one had the sensation of sitting on a cold wet slab. Being the youngest, I came first in the assembly line, but all six of us eventually progressed to sit in cotton nightshirts, drying our hair in front of the kitchen fire.

Medicines for both humans and animals were lumped together on the same high shelf and, after baths were over, Mum lifted down a square yellow tin. This, according to its deceptive label, contained a brand of wonder lozenge that cured coughs, croup and consumption. Gathering us round her like a hen with worms for her chicks, Mum stood over us, ladling out great lumps of green gritty liquorice powder into cups of senna tea. We would have preferred the worms. To our young minds Saturday night without liquorice was the main attraction in marriage.

Anyone with a skin blemish was treated to a dose of brimstone in black treacle as a Saturday evening second course. The horses were sometimes given the same mixture and, as Mum used to say, 'Show me a horse with pimples'. Chilblains and sprains were vigorously treated with rubbing oil; the label on the bottle showing both horse and groom proved conclusively to Mum that it was intended for man and beast. Many an egg-bound hen was galvanised into frantic productivity for fear of receiving a second dose of Mum's Saturday brew; and if the worm tablets in the orange tin kept our big-boned Kentish sheep from liver fluke, they did the same for us. A passing vet had once pronounced my sister 'weakly', and thereafter she was dosed with blood-mixture and a patent food for feeble calves.

At dosing time Dad lit the hurricane lamp and took himself off to the stables. As the youngest, I had my liquorice first; so it seemed downright unjust that on the night of the rebellion mine was the only cup to be emptied. My usually submissive sister stood with lips shut tight, her flushed face turning interesting shades of mauve as she defied the hands that held her nose, after she had declared that death was preferable to liquorice. In the scrimmage the contents of the cup were flung across the table. There was a crack like breaking ice on a frozen pond, and paraffin seeped across the velvet table-cloth. With a speed that belied her size, Mum snatched the smoking lamp and ran from the kitchen to hurl it on to the wet cobbles in the yard. Firelit shadows crept across the beams of the ceiling, as we children waited in the sort of calm that lies in the eye of a hurricane. The tempest struck. Mum, with copper-stick in hand and retribution in her heart, sent all six of us trembling to our beds.

Justice had been satisfied, the candles taken down, and we lay rattling the knobs on our old brass bedstead. My sister sobbed from injured pride and a sore seat; I lay shivering with fear. Somewhere in our house that awful reptile was probably slithering around in search of her, because she had broken the lamp and set it free.

A more terrifying thought sent me scuttling out of bed, along the dark passage, down the back stairs and into the kitchen, unfamiliar now in the dull light of a hurricane lamp. Dad sat in the high-backed windsor chair and, almost incoherent, I scrambled to the safety of his knee. When words would come I warned him that, although my sister had caused the lamp to be broken, it was Mum who had smashed it. I knew that Dad would not want the snake to eat her,

because she was his friend. Only that week I had seen him kiss her in the barn.

Strangely he had no fears. He said the biggest snake in Kent was only half the length of his shepherd's crook, so it would be no match for our cottage-loaf-shaped Mum and could even get a dose of liquorice for its pains. To prove his point he reasoned that the whale-boned, armour-plated stays Mum always wore would deter a rhinoceros, much more a slithering little snake.

Mum emerged from the scullery, pink-cheeked, her cotton nightgown buttoned to the neck, carrying her stays. I implored her to wear them night and day. She promised that she would, then held me close to her comforting feather-bolster front.

When I crossed the yard in the morning, I passed the shattered lamp, its wick still coiled up, in a rainbow puddle. It was replaced by a brass affair which gave a flat uninteresting light. The kitchen lost its magic, and its menace, from that day. Medicines we had in plenty, but never again Mum's Saturday brew.

(Winter 1970)

A MEAL FOR ALL SEASONS

Chris Richards

Ask the average traveller what Cornwall spells out to him and, should he be hungry, the answer invariably will be cream teas or Cornish pasties. Well, there's little to go wrong with a delicious clotted-cream tea. We can all recall them as dreams of delight when eaten in a cottage garden under a summer sky, wasps and all.

But Cornish pasties? What has happened in their name conjures up nothing but

horror to genuine Cornish folk. Many a Celt has blanched when confronted with the Anglicised monstrosity of a savoury masquerading as a pasty. With a shudder they dissociate themselves from the glutinous mush lost in a leaden pastry coat. That this concoction has the audacity to pass itself off as the genuine article beyond the Tamar adds insult to injury.

My introduction to the art of pasty-making came early in life one dark winter's afternoon, many years ago. Next door to us, over the low garden wall, lived Lizzie and Nellie, two spry elderly ladies who never seemed to resent the intrusion and curiosity of an eight-year-old boy. No non-sense in these parts about cooking only being women's work, nor was I ever conscious of feeling 'under their feet'. Lizzie was a cuddly rotund figure who bowled round the village as if on wheels. Nellie was quite her opposite – a bean-pole of a woman who managed to avoid the customary stoop of old age.

They made an harmonious pair in their tiny kitchen working round each other without hindrance, and winter baking days were a joy to me. I was fixed up on a three-legged stool, my nose level with the top of the well-scrubbed table, with the warmth of the coal-fired range toasting me pleas-antly down one side. As the afternoon darkened the oil-lamps were lit, and in these auspicious surroundings I was initi-ated into the secrets of pasty-making with all the solemnity of an apprentice al-chemist.

Nellie attended to the filling, a serious business, as she lifted from the zinc meat cupboard a choice lump of skirt beef. She was not averse to belly pork if pushed by economic necessity, but she'd have no truck at all with minced beef – 'flavourless and useless' was her opinion. My eyes followed the deft fingers as she sliced, ever so finely, the meat into nail-sized pieces. The potatoes and onions received similar treatment, each being collected in a separa-ate bowl though they all appeared to merge into one as the stinging onion-juice brought tears to my eyes. Meanwhile, Lizzie took on the pastry-making, her territory being the other half of the table. Suet pastry was chosen if she was pushed for time, but short-crust was her preference. Attired in

(Brian Walker)

her flowery wrap-round pinafore, she plunged her plump arms into the sifted flour and began rubbing in the lard. Gentle plumes of flour dust rose and settled on her ample chest. In her enthusiasm to shower the table with the flour sifter my nose and eyebrows received a dusting, lighter than any snowstorm. All this preparation took some time, but normally time was a plenti-ful commodity.

A true Cornish pasty, let it be under-stood, is a main meal in itself, not to be trifled with, and bearing no relation to the mass-produced snack favoured by shops. For the pastry template, Lizzie lifted down from the dresser a large dinner plate which she positioned and cut round with preci-sion. The rolling-pin flashed and remoulded the trimmings until six floured discs waited expectantly on the table top. The next bit was crucial and I was admonished to take particular care, for assembly of the ingre-dients must be authentic. First, a layer of potato, followed by swede if used. Next a most generous layer of onions, and, finally, the meat layer atop. Each layer was well seasoned with deft flicks of the wrists, salt in one hand and pepper in the other. A small dab of fat was secreted in the corner to ensure a moist result.

Carefully the pastry was folded over and the join crimped. This was a pleating and rolling action, born of years of practice and defying any mechanical imitation. Small steam holes completed the pasties before the tops were glazed and into the hot oven they went. A quarter of an hour later an appetising smell seeped into the kitchen, and Nellie armed herself with the fire-tongs. With a fine sense of ritual she attacked the range with a great deal of clatter to close down the dampers and so reduce the heat for a further hour's cooking time. The result was stupendous. A cross-section of the pasty revealed the contents still retaining their stratified composition, with the vegetables done to a turn in the descending juices of the meat.

From such attention to detail families adapted their pasties for personal preference – more of this and less of that – and an identifying pattern of steam holes proved an ingenious way of ensuring the right pasty reached the right person. Larger families made gigantic pasties to be baked in a roasting tin. They were sliced according to appetite and made a welcome substitute for a meat roast in times of hardship.

I never forgot the lessons of Lizzie and Nellie, nor their cosy kitchen, and indeed there was a sequel about two years after my initiation. At the ripe age of ten years I took on the ladies of the village in the home-cooking competition at the chapel bazaar. Little did I realise the uproar I was to cause. Under the Cornish pasty section, I tendered my offering, feeling justifiably proud of the gleaming savoury. With the brashness of youth I was not too surprised to hear that it had earned first prize, but I still rushed off to the chapel tin hut to confirm my success. It was true enough! The first-prize red ticket could not be mistaken beneath my entry, but I was somewhat bewildered by all the noise. Fifteen or twenty women were going at it hammer and tongs, making the corrugated iron roof ring with pandemonium. Apparently the village was now divided over the wretched question of glazing. Half were for it, but the others maintained it was *not traditional* and demanded that my pasty be disqualified *immediately*. The half maintaining that the custom was widespread, and that it was really a question of sour grapes, were losing ground. At which point Nellie entered the battle, her cheeks reddening with indignation. Reaching her full height she startled the onlookers by admitting she was almost eighty years old. (Gasps of incredulity.) Not only had she always glazed her pasties, but (she hammered home the message) so had her mother – and her mother's grandmother! So how old was tradition? Well, no one else was prepared to disclose her age, nor family background, and Nellie's intervention saved the day. The bright red card remained beneath my pasty and I skipped all the way home gleefully clutching the half-crown prize. Nellie, I was given to understand later, strode home filled with pride that her unusual male apprentice had somehow proved her reputation.

And now, years and years later, that first bite into a steaming pasty conjures up Cornish summers and winters. Summers, warm and thrift-scented on the cliff-tops, sitting beside Lizzie as I almost drowsed with the endless motion of the translucent sea. Until a none-too-gentle nudge would rouse me as Lizzie pointed out the Atlantic rollers breaking leisurely on the shore. 'Watch how the waves curl over and run along the crest – see you copy nature's action and you can't fail to make a good seal on your pasties.' So now you know.

(Spring 1983)

ROOM AT THE INN

William Gooding

'There's six boats coming in from the moors,' I said to Father on a winter's evening. From our inn I could gaze across the flood-waters of Tealham Moor where the small lights, bobbing like fireflies, were zigzagging nearer. Half a dozen customers in flat boats lit by hurricane latterns were coming to spend the evening.

Overheard the painted sign of grouse and pheasant creaked on its hinges, and the light of the door lanterns reflected the gold in the tail feathers of the cock. Nearby, for dry-land customers, there were mounting steps and a great iron half-hoop for tethering horses. The boatmen would drive iron spikes and chains into the grass bank at the bottom of the hill to anchor their craft.

'Put the iron pokers in the fire, Willie.' Father, who was serving home-made cider at fourpence a pint, knew all his customers. 'And get out the canister of ginger. They'll want it mulled tonight. And put a fresh loaf on the bar. Maybe they'll want toast in it.'

The pokers would be red-hot, the two-handled pints of cider ready laced with ginger, by the time the chilled boatmen came. Into the cider would go the flaming poker, making it hiss and rear up in a spiral of white froth and fragrance, and the broken toast would follow into the steaming brew.

'Ah, 'tis a good drink,' said George, our oldest customer, ''twould drive the chill out o' a corpse.'

The whitewashed Somerset inn was at the top of the hill. On warm summer days the cider mugs stood outside on the broad shelf of the half-door. The long low walls were covered with pink roses in season and decorated by the pronged spears of the eel-fishers, the tall black hedge-nets of the starling-catchers and the decoy traps of the goldfinch-cagers. An immense orchard lay to the side. The walled garden was lined with greengages, Victorias and loganberries, and from the bar window customers might see water being winched from the well in an old oak bucket.

The inn was also a general store, a place of sale and barter, and in the wet season an unofficial *poste restante* for letters which could not be delivered over the floods. Letters were rare but always hoped for: 'Biss thee got a letter for I this marnin'?' If so, it would be stuck between two cider jugs on the shelf. Father would hand it over and, often enough, give a hand with the reading.

The shop, an old stone-flagged store next to the bar, was filled with the odour of corn and candles, tea, spice and bacon. A row of iron-hard scarlet Edam cheeses stood on an upper shelf. If a customer was so pinched as to want but half, Father would cleave it with an axe kept for the purpose.

'Han't thee got no Zalmon's tea?'

This was highly prized by boatmen and landlubbers alike, being the first product ever to give coupons for prizes. There was no substitute. 'Us'll wait. Missus 'll drink watter firrst.'

The shopping was sometimes packed in a basket, but more often into a scarlet kerchief big as a bedspread. This was first removed from neck or knees, spread on the counter as groceries were pell-melled in, then knotted at the corners round a stick which took it to the waiting boat.

In the bar, with its huge fireplace and two oak settles at one end, the old beam was

'The bar, with its old beam, fireplace and two oak settles . . .' (Brian Walker)

clustered with brilliantly shined horse-brasses. Copper bowls filled with marigolds and nasturtiums stood in the windows, and sometimes an old blue jug with Cheddar pinks. There was an ancient hurdy-gurdy and a shove-ha'penny board: these and muzzle-loading took up most of the evenings. Brass powder-horns came from huge gaming-pockets, and the rammers rhythmically packed home the powder, while smoke rose to the ceiling and conversation on seasons, markets and harvests burred on.

The spiral stair went round the chimney-piece. Every evening I took my scrubbed night-face and my candlestick through the bar on my way to bed and was greeted by a chorus of: 'Goodnight, Willie my zonner! Sleep well!'

My bed was above the bar. Lamplight filtered through gaps in the rafters; mingled fragrance of mulled cider and tobacco caressed my nostrils. The clang of mugs, the tinkle of the hurdy-gurdy, tumbling ha'pennies, the talk in rich rolling Somerset usually sent me off to sleep soundly; but occasionally I would put an eye to the widest crack in the boards. Below might be a wild duck or teal waiting for a swop, or pale green duck-eggs in a basket of rushes, cheek by jowl with a dead rabbit or hare. Pigeon, snipe and partridge found their way in, and once only I spotted a bunch of larks, legs tied together. Father, shocked, turned the gypsy away with 'Us likes our larks to sing round here'.

Bartering went on endlessly. Out of the boats came gigantic white celery streaked with black peat soil, dinner-plate-sized mushrooms, clutches of peewit's eggs and black floury potatoes: 'Who'll buy my chiddies? Six shillin' a hundred.' He would be a while selling them. These were the 'twenties when money was scarce.

Auctions were a different matter. 'Who'll bid me for this fine hayrick?' called for carefully counted cash or the rarer cheque book. They took place in the afternoons and were improved by a pint of cider or, occasionally, a beer. Beer was a poor second, and we sold no spirits. Cider was king.

Sunday mornings in our inn saw a two-handled quart mug being filled with cider and passed from man to man, each taking a quaff. The mugs always bore the entwined wheatsheaf and plough device and the old verse, often jovially recited aloud:

Let the wealthy and great
Roll in splendour and state;
I envy them not, I declare it.
I rear my own lamb,
My own chickens and ham;
I sheer my own fleece and I wear it.
I have lawns, I have bowers,
I have fruit, I have flowers,
The lark is my morning alarmer.
So, jolly boys, now
Here's God speed the plough,
Long life and success to the farmer.

The cider-making house behind the bar was large, dark and impregnated with the smell of fermenting apples. Hogsheads stood in rows, some unbunged and topped with wooden funnels, others runnelled as through by a white creeping lava which poured in ferment down their sides to the floor. The press, filled with pomace, was in the middle. Every couple of days, as the pomace squeezed out, Father would cut round it with a hay-knife and clap it back on top under the screw. When it was dry, the wheatstraw was taken carefully away to be used again and the dry pulp was shovelled into farm carts. Cows loved it mixed with bran.

All day, in our green-apple harvests, tall empty baskets beckoned in the orchard.

(Brian Walker)

They ended my mole-catching revenues. I liked to sit with penknife and barrel-stave making a snare, threading the six holes with copper wire and a long switch of pliable ground ash, then setting it with muddied hands in a field on the way to school. But this and the joys of fishing, and of riding cart-horses out to distant pastures for pennies, faded away before those apple baskets.

'Willie,' was the cry, 'what are you wasting time on? Get into the orchard.'

GOING TO VISIT RELATIONS

Meant a second scrubbing of bare
    knees,
White shirt Sunday-best decorum
Not kicking stones with new shoes,
Close inspection on arrival,
Pedigree likenesses seen,

Straight-backed polished mahogany
    chairs
The prickle-fidget of horsehair,
Affectionate force-feeding, fruit cake
Good manners couldn't reject,
The time when I was sick,

At last getting out of the parlour,
Following the men to feed calves,
Their inquisitive sandpaper tongues,
Tracking a hen's egg-laying cackle,
A goodbye half-crown in my hand.
                    Tom Rawling (Spring 1984)

When it was not apples it was hogsheads. They needed cleaning for the new cider. Last year's sludge was poured out to nourish the apple trees. Drunken ducks flapped and cavorted riotously round me while I scrubbed and swilled out barrels with fresh spring water.

Morgan Sweets, the earliest apples, made the thinnest and least popular cider. Later, mixed crops of Warner King, Tom Putt, Horslyn and Ribstone Black made a fuller better-flavoured drink. Father's cider was a simple matter of apple juice and brown sugar, but our bar held gilders of lilies: 'I be puttin' a raw leg o' lamb in each o' my hogsheads thissen year', or 'I be puttin' a bottle o' brandy in a special hogshead every year till me boy be twenty-one'. But, good or bad, all went down.

(Spring 1966)

MY APPRENTICESHIP

William Gooding

The craftsman peered up the bole of the elm. 'Ay, farmer, I'll take it.' The tree was at Elm Tree Farm, Heathhouse, on a knoll overlooking the flat Somerset moors, intersected by rhines, where every year the River Brue flooded on its slow course to the sea at Highbridge. Thomas Edney, the craftsman, beckoned to me, his fifteen-year-old apprentice: 'See, William? The tree is good – no knots, straight boughs. We'll have it down now.'

Those were peaceful country years. The Second World War was far enough off to be discounted. About us were the heavy dairy farms with substantial Georgian houses. The villages of Mark, Blackford and Wedmore lay like the spokes of a wheel; and the bluish Mendip ridge, with the great Cheddar Gorge, formed a low protecting spine behind us. While other wheelwrights and smiths were installing steam-driven machinery and electricity, Thomas Edney's shop remained an obstinate oasis of handcraftsmanship. The smithy and workshop, a long span-roofed building, stood only a short distance from the farm. Its double doors, open to all winds and weathers, were like huge abstract canvasses, from the cleanings and primings of many brushes. 'Hurry up, boy! Get this lot clean!' the old man would command. Completely content, I would scrub whorls, noughts, crosses, zigzags and cartoon faces until the brushes were dry of paint.

At the shop the elm trunk was hand sawn into rough blocks. Holes were then drilled through the centres to allow air to pass into the heart of the wood, to prevent radial cracking. It was my job to pile the blocks in a quiet corner on intersecting slats to dry out for a year. Meanwhile we got on with the turning of matured blocks into wheelhubs. Every day I scrambled up a rickety ladder to the half-platform in the rafters which housed the six-foot wooden wheel connected by a belt to an ancient lathe below. To a chorus of 'Keep it going, boy. Don't go to sleep up there', Thomas Edney deftly turned the blocks. All around, in neat array, were cleft oak spokes, also shaped by his hand. In the adjoining smithy the bonds were being forged. Bonding day was an exciting occasion with a high accident rate. The red-hot iron bond was taken out to the assembled hub, spokes and ash rim, hammered into position round the wheel, then instantly contracted under the hissing steam as buckets of cold water were thrown over it.

The work was mostly seasonal and, as in any other trade, we kept ahead of demand. 'Floods 'll be up soon, boy. We'll get half a dozen flat-bottomed boats ready.' These, at £5 apiece, were made from green pliable elm. I would sit sorting out properly angled wood for the ribs. When assembled, the boat was turned keel uppermost and, amid smoke and anvil sparks, we applied pitch to every joint. Later I would have the job of floating the boat out on to the water. Sometimes, too, there was the pleasure of lying in the bottom to watch the wild geese go over and, on rare occasions, a pot shot at wild duck with a muzzle-loader.

During the winter we did a great deal of tree-felling. Then the midday meal consisted of a whole loaf of bread, a pound of Cheddar cheese, hacked by Thomas Edney, with far less than his usual skill, from the body of a truckle, and often a whole shoulder of cold mutton, all washed down with cold tea, as we sat on a fallen tree trunk. On wet or quiet days I turned the old paint-mill at the back of the shop, pouring red lead, turpentine and linseed oil into it and grinding them smooth. Or, for hours, I would sandpaper panels of the kitchen dressers for which we were noted, until I felt I could truthfully answer the inevitable question: 'Like silk is it, boy? Like silk?' Sometimes I would be set to making iron-ringed hammers of apple wood, popular in the district for smashing coal and peat turves. And the arrival of the eels in the river coincided with the finishing off of the ash handles for five-pronged eel spears made by the smith.

Summer brought a high tide of activity:

'Sharing the excitement of cider-making . . .' (Brian Walker)

rakes, loaders and hand-made wains had to be ready for haymaking. There were cheese presses and butter churns for the milk flush, and apple mills for the cider harvest. The wains, with traditionally blue bodies and red wheels, were made of three woods: oak for the frame, elm for the bodywork and tough ash for the curving front panel. From the local inns and cider-making farms the cry would go up: 'The pumace isn't coming'. Often this meant an enjoyable time away from the shop, sharing the excitement of cider-making, while presses were being repaired. For me there was usually a lot of waiting about, and I would be told, 'Help yourself'. Then, sitting on a pile of straw, I would insert a long wheat straw into the trough and, in the warmth and goldness of the day, syphon up sweet unfermented apple juice.

Chief joy of the lunch-hour break was a visit to Mrs Tincknell's shop down the road. Its leaded bow window was almost obliterated by the huge jar of bees' wine for sale at a penny a glass. She had a kind heart for apprentices and schoolboys; and I would return without a care in the world, soothed for the price of threepence by an outsize apple dumpling from the shop oven and two tumblers of alcoholic bees' wine.

Occasionally Thomas Edney went to Bridgwater. He would return with fresh tools, a new leather hide for wheel-washers and half a dozen kegs of paint powder; and his white hair and beard, grown so patriarchal since the previous trip, would have been severely pruned. Every seventh day he laid aside his white carpenter's apron, the ancient paint-decorated hat and the gaming coat with massive pockets. Putting on a black suit and gold chain, he went to the nearby chapel where he was the local preacher. Under pain of royal displeasure I also attended three times on Sunday; and each year I received a book inscribed in the familiar copperplate: 'For regular attendance at Heathhouse Sunday school'. On Monday morning I was asked: 'Did you enjoy my sermon?' 'Yes, sir,' I would reply, upon which we would settle to work.

Thomas Edney was an inveterate hummer and whistler of hymn tunes. I would find myself swinging the plane in time to the slow cadence of 'Jesu, Lover of My Soul', only to be shaken by its sharp cessation and the command: 'Smarten up, boy! You'll never be finished'. 'If only he would try

'Thomas Edney was sitting by his workshop door alone.' (Brian Walker)

"Onward Christian Soldiers" or "Fight the Good Fight",' I complained to the smith, 'I'd get on better.'

When the fifth spring arrived, my apprenticeship years were up. Looking over the moors, I felt I could stay for ever. The floods had gone. The farmer-mariners, who daily paddled their flat-bottomed boats to smithy, stores, inn or chapel, had drawn them up for the dry season. The local boys were at their favourite games of rhine-jumping, swimming in the calm Brue and hunting peewits' eggs. But the prospect of learning draughtsmanship at Merchant Venturers in Bristol beckoned. It was time to go.

On the last day, wage in pocket, I took the short road home. At the corner I looked back. Thomas Edney was sitting by his workshop door alone. He had picked up a carborundum stone and, white head bent, was meticulously sharpening the points of a fine hand-saw.

(Winter 1964)

CASUAL LABOUR

Peter Finch

Nothing about casual labour is so casual as the method of its recruitment. One school holiday I was discussing the prospects of harvest work with my brother, who had been taken on at the outset. His farm already had a sufficient labour force, he told me, but 'Owd Herb ain't too wrapped up in ut'. Owd Herb was the farmer. Next day I ambled into his stackyard and, sitting on a bale, watched him jab the sheaves of wheat as they were pitched up from the trolley and toss them over to the stacker in a half-filled bay of the dutch barn. The trolley emptied, he leant on his fork and gazed down at me, wondering whether the skinny youngster were man enough for the task. 'Comen' up?' he asked at length. 'If y' loike,' I replied.

I climbed the ladder on to the stack, and he descended and wandered off to the farmhouse. A few minutes later his son John showed not the slightest surprise at my presence as, without a word, he brought a fresh load into the yard, drew it up to the stack, unhooked, backed round to the empty trolley, hooked in and trundled off down the lane again. The ropes were untied and I started where Owd Herb had left off, without a word of greeting or instruction from the lad unloading the trolley or from the wizened little stacker, with both of whom I was acquainted.

My position was regularised when John said to me a few days later: 'I s'pose you're keepen' count of your hours?' I nodded. No further bargaining was necessary, and indeed even that was superfluous. I knew I could trust Owd Herb to pay me a fair wage, and he knew I would not desert him till the job was done. Eventually, when the harvest was finished he was informed by a devious route that I had ninety-six hours to my credit. Shortly afterwards I received an envelope whose contents, erring on the side of generosity, approximated as closely as bank-notes could to my entitlement at the prevailing rate.

(Summer 1957)

Wheelwrights at work in Little Barrington. (Roy Dixon)

THE WORKING WORLD

LEARNING THE DRILL . . .

Chris Wait

The cowman and I started the hand-milking a little earlier in the mornings during the hectic month of April. It was my first year as 'boy' on that small Surrey farm, back in the 1950s, and I was employed where the boss thought I would be most useful or, as the cowman frequently reminded me, where I could do the least harm.

The boss usually came into the stall

halfway through milking, bubbling over with plans for the day's work, and sent me straight out to help Fred, the carter. It took two of us to lift the two-hundredweight sacks of seed and fertiliser on to the iron-wheeled, flat, turntable waggon called 'the trolley'. Ernie had a grumble about being left to milk on his own, but he realised the importance of getting the drilling done while the weather held.

'Shall I ask him if I can stay and help you finish?' I asked. 'No, boy,' he said. 'Do like 'e says. I can manage better wi'out you under me feet. An' anyways, I can see you be a-bustin' to be out in them fields.'

The ground had been given its final harrowing, either with the tractor, or with the two horses nodding their heads across the field in the old, proud way, with Fred stumbling over the clods behind, and we got busy with the drill. We had a new drill that year. The boss was tired of mending our old horse-drawn, Massey-Harris, seed-only machine. He had converted it for the tractor, and the headlong, four miles-an-hour of the Fordson was too much for it. It kept falling to pieces and holding us up. So, after a cautious visit to his bank manager, the boss ordered a brand-new 'Sunshine' combine drill.

'It's the latest thing, Fred,' he said proudly. 'It puts the seed and fertiliser in, all in one go. It'll save us hours.'

Fred wasn't impressed. 'What you means, Boss, is that it's one more job that won't be done proper-like, wi' 'orses, but tear-arsin' about wi' that bliddy tractor.'

'Silly old fool,' said the boss. 'He doesn't realise we've got to keep up with the times.' But he waited until Fred was out of earshot. He didn't like to offend the old man.

The drill was delivered, in all the glory of its new paintwork, and we left it out by the road for the neighbours to marvel at for a

'As we went through the field gate I heard a tinkling noise . . .'
(Anne Roper)

couple of hours, then the boss took it up the lane to the field we were going to drill. I rode on the varnished footboard on the back of the drill, and just as we went through the field gate I heard a tinkling noise and noticed that the shoe of one of the coulters was dragging loose. We stopped and examined it.

'Look at this!' said the boss. 'Blasted nut's come undone. They can't have tightened it up properly at the factory.'

We checked the rest of the coulters and found that they were *all* loose. And more than that – every nut and bolt on the machine was slack. The bumpy quarter of a mile up the lane had nearly shaken the thing to pieces. The reason was obvious – there wasn't a single spring-washer anywhere.

There was no point in tightening up the loose nuts without washers, as they would have come loose again in a few minutes, so I was dispatched to scour the village for spring-washers. 'Go to the garage, the builder's yard and the blacksmith's. And get a shift on – I want to get some corn in today.'

I sped back up the lane, panting on my

bike, my pockets bulging with spring-washers and all the spanners I could lay my hands on, and we got to work. We took off every nut and bolt on that machine, put spring-washers on and tightened everything up properly. It took a couple of hours. We were just finishing when Fred came down the lane leading the two horses. He stopped to have a gloat.

'Whoever made that 'chine that way, boy?' he asked me. I read the maker's label. 'Sunshine Sundrill, made in Australia,' I announced.

'Ar, that'll be it then, you,' said Fred.

'They don't unnerstan' mechanicals out there, boy. It be all sheep an' kang'roos an' rabbits an' that.' He turned to leer evilly at the boss who had just crawled out from under the drill. 'I finished my job wi' the horses, Boss, an' I 'spect you'll soon be a-startin' wi' that time-savin', wunnerful new drill.' The old man winked at me and spat thoughtfully on the ground. 'Damme if that 'aven't saved you some time today, Boss!'

The boss made no reply. He couldn't think of one.

(Spring 1985)

LAKELAND LIVERING

Roland Wade

When the tenant retired last spring, I bought Long House Farm, in the upper reaches of the Duddon valley, for reletting to the tenant of my adjoining Tongue House Farm. This involved a 'livering': the delivery of the landlord's flock of heafed sheep by Bill Routledge, the outgoing tenant, to Lake District Farm Estates, who handed them over to me, to pass on to my tenant, Dennis Williamson. Most hill-sheep farms in the Lake District have a flock owned by the landlord and let to the tenant with the farm – a custom apparently confined to this and some adjoining hill districts. The flock has a fixed number of sheep, and they are divided into categories: ewes, tups, twinters and hoggs. An outgoing tenant must hand back this number. Any sheep in excess of it are his own.

These farms depend on the open fells for their grazing, and the 'heafed' flock – the flock that will always return to its 'heaf' or its own part of the fell – is an essential feature. Long House Farm heaf is on part of the Coniston fells, where as many as twenty farms have flocks grazing. Each keeps substantially to its own heaf, although there are no fences. If a tenant sold off the flock it would be difficult to build up another, for sheep brought from any local farm would go straight back to their own heaf. One farmer told me that to get a new flock heafed would involve shepherding every day for a year. If foot-and-mouth disease had come and his flock had been slaughtered, he would have given up sheep farming.

The origin of the landlord's flock is uncertain. It may have been a means of ensuring that the flock was maintained, though in other parts of the country there are heafed flocks owned by tenants. Or it may reflect past difficulty in finding a tenant

Long House Farm in the upper reaches of the Duddon Valley. (G. V. Berry)

with capital enough to buy the flock from the outgoing tenant. It is no innovation. A conveyance of Long House Farm in 1836 not only conveyed the land and buildings to the purchaser, but also assigned and transferred 'All that and those the stock or flock of heath-bred and heath-going sheep consisting of 74 hogs or yearling sheep and 255 older sheep heath-bred and heath-going upon the said premises or upon the commons within the Manor of Dunnerdale-with-Seathwaite'.

For the livering each party has two 'viewers' – local sheep farmers who count and check the flock and settle any differences as to quality. There is no short cut from old tenant to new. So the Long House livering involved eight viewers: two each for Bill Routledge and his landlord, for me and my tenant. Livering day was fixed for the last Saturday in March. But first Bill Routledge had to gather the sheep from the fells and sort them to get the right number of each category. The Long House landlord's flock consisted of 469 sheep:

> 70 gimmer hoggs
> 40 wether hoggs
> 60 gimmer twinters
> 30 wether twinters
> 6 rams
> 263 ewes

Two or three days were needed to gather and sort them.

Livering started with the ewes, which had been put in a small garth adjoining the farmhouse. First, to save time, they were counted by all the viewers together. After two counts had both produced the correct number, each party's viewers checked over the ewes for quality. Occasionally one would reach out his crook to catch a ewe round the neck and draw it out of the flock. 'Nay, tha can't liver yon laal thing,' said one; and off it would go with one of the lads a-straddle, to be replaced by another from the surplus sheep. Only seven were rejected.

The first two pairs of viewers – one for Bill Routledge and one for Lake District Farm Estates – then went off to count and check twenty gimmer hoggs penned in a small barn. (Hoggs are lambs in their first winter.) The rest were away 'wintering' at the coast or in some other softer clime. As soon as the gimmer hoggs had been accepted by the second pair of viewers, mine joined them to take over for me as buyer of the farm. The process of counting and checking was repeated. Then came Dennis Williamson's viewers, to complete the take-over.

The first viewers had meanwhile moved on to start on the wether hoggs in another building; then on to the wether twinters (lambs in their second winter), to the gimmer twinters and to the tups, until the whole landlord's flock had been counted and checked over by the first two pairs of viewers. All the time the others were following on, re-counting and checking until Dennis Williamson had accepted the whole flock apart from the wintering hoggs. They would be taken over later.

Viewing papers, giving the number and quality of each category of sheep, were then signed by all the viewers, and a signed copy was taken by each party. Dennis Williamson marked all the sheep in the landlord's flock with a dab of green paint to identify them. A future gathering might bring in from the fell the odd few which had been missed and would still belong to Bill Routledge.

We adjourned to the farmhouse, where the womenfolk had been busy preparing a tea worthy of the occasion. After the meal some of the viewers and helpers started to drift away, but for others it was a time to linger: a livering does not come every day. Drinks were brought out, Lakeland hunting songs were sung and reminiscences were plentiful. Not until the early hours of Sunday morning did the last of the viewers depart. A good livering, all agreed.

(Summer 1969)

Bill Routledge (right) with waiting viewers. (G. V. Berry)

END OF THE ROAD

Peter Rosser

'Ah reckon that'll fettle it,' the plumber said as he smeared a little paste round the union joint that had wept on the kitchen floor. 'Fettle' suggested a foreigner in Hampshire. 'Ay,' he answered. 'There were nowt for me in Millom. As far as me and me mates could find there were nowt in all Cumberland, and yer soon gets tired o' laikin' [idling].'

One morning in May 1920 he had set off to walk to Southampton, sleeping in haystacks and hedges. He counted it his greatest fortune that he had been issued with a new pair of boots shortly before his discharge from the army. If he found no work on the way, he would sail abroad.

'Ah thowt t' little towns 'ud be t' likely places, so Ah didn't mek straight for Southampton. Ah had more of a sally-round like, knockin' and askin' all t' way. Ah give all as asked "What can you do?" t' same answer: "Work". Three days was most as Ah ever got from one master; but it were same for all. Never lacked for company. Walk a bit, sit a bit, wi' t' birds to tell yer it were bedtime. There were plenty about like yersen if yer wanted a bit of a camp [chat].'

The sally-round took him through Odiham where the sign 'W. Boyce, Builder', clouded by rambler roses, was spotted by an eye sharpened on long empty-bellied miles. 'It were end o' t' road for me, July 1920 – fifteenth o' July. Don't know why Ah remembers t' date, but Ah do. "Right," he says to me, "Start seven tomorrow. Fortnight's trial".'

'And you've been working for the same firm ever since?' It was W. Boyce, Builder, who was attending to our boiler. 'Well,' the plumber admitted with North Country caution, 'He ain't said no more abaht it.'

(Spring 1970)

EDWARDIAN GARDENER

George William Young

As a small boy in my native Essex I had always wanted to take up gardening on the grand scale. I had to leave school at the age of eleven, when my parents could no longer afford to pay my twopence a week to the British School – I was the fourth of a family of ten – and spent some years doing odd jobs about the village. When I was about fifteen a Quaker farmer sent me for two terms to the horticultural college at Chelmsford, where I was awarded a first-class Royal Horticultural Society certificate.

My first place, Trueloves at Ingatestone, where I started as a garden boy about 1893, was not exactly a stately home; but it was a beginning. There I lived in with two other young gardeners, and during that time I had my first experience of cooking. Each of us took one week in three, and there was much rivalry to see who could come nearest to mother at home. I made my first Yorkshire pudding in a tin saucer used to stand plants in, and baked my first cake in a small flower-pan well lined with greaseproof paper.

It was an unwritten law that a youth should have learnt all he could in one place after two years, and I progressed to a job as under-gardener at Boreham House near Chelmsford. Then, after another two years, I went as first journeyman to Blendon Hall in Kent. This meant that I was qualified to do a lot of work on my own and could hope one day to become a head with several men under me. While I was at Blendon, only a few miles from London, Queen Victoria died and I went to see the funeral. I was much impressed by the number of crowned heads following on horseback and by the ladies in their carriages draped from head to toe in crape; for all you could see of them, it was difficult to tell whether they were human or just rolls of crape.

The author at Welbeck, 1904.

Soon after Edward VII succeeded to the throne, I landed a job as foreman to the head gardener at Welbeck Abbey, home of the Duke and Duchess of Portland. He told me on arrival that he would not be seeing much of me, as I would be 'the Duchess's man', in charge of three large conservatories, of an underground glass-roofed corridor and of all the floral decorations in the Abbey. The conservatories, built in the style of the Crystal Palace, were about 20 ft high and contained some very large camellias, palms, eucalyptuses and other exotics. Two or three men were required to carry them into the house. The corridor, about 16 ft wide and 100 yds long, contained groups of flowering plants, including specimen fuchsias and geraniums, which were renewed every two weeks from the glasshouses. It led directly from the picture gallery, which was 157 ft by 64 ft and all underground, its flat roof being covered with shrubs; it was sometimes used as a ballroom. The corridor itself made a pleasant promenade, with seats among the flowers, soft lighting and fountains. From it an underground passage led to the Riding School over a distance of 1070 yds.

The death of Queen Victoria made a great difference to the way of life of England's upper classes, including their manner of dress. Away went the ladies' prim bonnets in favour of large brimmed hats trimmed with coils of feathers and flowers. The hair was now brushed out and up into a fuzzy mass. Feather boas were worn about two yards long, thrown over one shoulder. The men discarded their top hats in favour of King Edward's favourite headgear, the trilby, cocked jauntily to one side. There were extravagant house parties. At dinner parties both ladies and gentlemen wore flowers, and at Welbeck it fell to me to make up buttonholes for the men and sprays for the ladies. For the buttonholes colour did not matter a great deal; a single carnation or rose-bud would serve. The sprays were a very different matter. I found it best to consult the lady's-maid about the colour of the dress her mistress was going to wear. The most favoured flowers were carnations, lilies of the valley, roses and orchids, and sometimes Parma violets of a soft Wedgwood blue.

The Duchess, who nearly always wore the large pale pink carnation named after her, was very fond of flowers. Besides the pot plants in all the main rooms, she liked to have cut flowers on the table at breakfast and lunch as well as at dinner. When the party included royalty there might be as many as forty guests round a table some thirty-five feet long. It was the custom for the heads of departments to bring their friends to see the room just before the Duchess arrived to arrange the place-names, and during one of the visits of King Edward and Queen Alexandra this nearly caused a disaster. I had spent a long time doing the table and was rather proud of the effect. Then, just before dinner-time, one of the onlookers, in trying to smell a flower, pulled the whole arrangement over so that the water spilt on the cloth. Checking the rising panic, I sent all available people to the rose garden to pick as many heads as they could in five minutes. Meanwhile I took all the flowers from the table, removed the heads and arranged these flat on the cloth, following the meandering pattern of the spilt water. With the hastily gathered rose heads I made several other smaller patterns on either side, finishing just as the meal was announced. The following morning, when I was told that Her Grace wanted to see me, I thought I was in for a carpeting. She said: 'Her Majesty wishes me to congratulate you on the lovely table you did last night, and I too congratulate

you. I think it was the best I have ever seen.' I tried several times to repeat the effect, but found that I was always making a set pattern rather than a natural one such as the spilt water had formed.

At this time, it must be remembered, there were many more crowned heads in Europe than there are today. Most of them were related by blood or marriage to Edward VII, and Welbeck took its share in entertaining them on state and private visits, for both the Duke and Duchess held appointments in the Royal Household. Among the visits I chiefly remember was that of the King and Queen of Portugal, as they were the most carefully guarded of any. My duties took me to the royal apartments once, and sometimes twice, daily. To reach them I had to answer three challenges and, as I entered, a plain-clothes detective accompanied me and watched my every movement, though to outward appearance he was just anxious to pick up tips about flower arrangement. History records the reason for so much care. A bomb thrown into the royal carriage as it left Lisbon station blew the king, queen, horses and outriders sky high.

It was at Welbeck that I had my first ride in a motor-car – an Arrol Johnston with two seats back to back as in the horse-drawn dog-cart. The tyres were of solid rubber. The only protection from the weather was a leather apron for each seat. The engine, which was under the seats, was started by a sharp pull on a rope, as with some lawn-mowers today. I saw one of the first motor speed trials at Clipstone, when the unheard-of speed of 25 to 30 m.p.h. was recorded. About 1904 a large number of cars toured England, led by Prince Henry of Prussia; and while the drivers halted at Welbeck for rest and refreshment I took photographs of the cars parked in the yard. For protection a man could wear his cloth

Cars parked in the timber yard at Welbeck Abbey.

cap with the peak at the back, but the ladies had to tie down their large hats with unbecoming motoring scarves. Bicycles, which had made such strides in design that it had become quite the thing for heads of great houses to ride around on them, soon lost status when the car made its appearance.

After six happy and instructive years at Welbeck I left to take a place as a married man. I was appointed estate manager and head gardener to Sir Charles and Lady Ellis, who had recently acquired Rampton Manor near Retford. Both were keen gardeners and wished to alter and extend

the gardens and pleasure grounds. We took in a large strip of parkland and a piece of rough ground on the edge of a pine wood, where we planted many shrubs and some beautiful lesser-known conifers, and made a rock garden, a rose garden and large herbaceous borders, each with plants of a single colour range. My favourite was the 'grey' border, which included lavender, carnations and globe artichokes. Laburnums formed a shady walk from the house to the church and village; under them we planted polyanthuses, which did well there. We raised many seedlings from selected plants, and one year, when we exhibited a group at the R. H. S. Hall, I smuggled in a little first-year plant for which I had a special fancy. It won an award of merit, and we worked up quite a number from it; but the outbreak of war put a stop to all that.

Nineteen-fourteen saw the beginning of the decline of the great estates. In their heyday they enabled the rich to live in a style becoming to their station in society. A really large establishment was self-contained, with its own chapel, school, post office, fire brigade and water and sewage works. The women on the indoor staff would include the housekeeper, lady's-maid, two still-room maids, sewing maid, linen maid, ten or twelve housemaids, five or six laundry maids and two kitchen maids. On the male side there would be a steward, clerk, valet, wine butler, plate butler, three or four footmen and cellar men, several odd men to carry coal and so on, a chef, kitchen porter, vegetable cook, baker and assistant. A groom of the chambers was responsible for keeping all the writing tables clean and supplied, and for seeing that nothing of a confidential nature was left in writing or on blotting paper. He also saw to the supply of newspapers and periodicals, and dealt with all incoming and outgoing mail. Outdoors there might be thirty-five gardeners, not to mention stable and farm employees. A maid servant would be paid about £10 a year, an indoor manservant perhaps £30, and a gardener or groom £1 a week.

It is often said that the great houses have been taxed out of existence, but I think it was the disappearance of a plentiful supply of cheap domestic labour which caused so many of them to be given up. Of those where I worked two have been pulled down; the site of one is built over, and the other is covered with caravans. Two are military colleges, one has been converted into luxury flats, another into a girls' school. A large business firm uses one for entertaining overseas customers, and the last is a children's home.

(Winter 1968)

VICTORIAN BUSINESS WOMAN

Ann Barton

When my great-grandfather John Lewis returned to England after some adventurous years with gold prospectors in Australia, he found it difficult to settle down in quiet north-east Essex. His life had been tough and exacting, first as an apprentice serving in the coastal barges of a Colchester owner, then in the fruit and wine boats that sailed to Spain. It was a cattle boat that took him to Australia, where he left the sea and drove wagons carrying prospectors to the gold-fields of Coolgardie. He seems to have acquired some gold himself; but the story goes that his partner absconded with a large part of it. He returned home without a fortune.

John was now about thirty-five, in the year 1860. Having celebrated his homecoming with a party at the Ardleigh railway tavern, he married the prettiest girl in the neighbourhood. Sarah Bloice lived at Burnt Heath with her Aunt Keeble, a very respectable lady who warned her niece against marriage with the wild young man. But John dazzled the girl with his stories of a world of which she knew nothing. Besides, his father owned property in the Tendring Hundred, a not unimportant consideration to an orphan girl with ambition.

The couple took over a bakery business in Mistley, but that was too regular a life for the sailor-adventurer. Next they moved to the White House, owned by John's father, on the Colchester-Bromley road. This small country house with stables and paddocks was suitable for the business of pony and donkey dealing; but John lived a highly irregular life, drinking spirits to excess with his clients and becoming quarrelsome when Sarah remonstrated. One night, returning late, he replied to her protestations by gathering up the feather bed with her in it and throwing the whole bundle downstairs.

In the meantime his parents had died, and he began to dissipate the rents which came from the properties. So Sarah, determined that the future of her nine-year-old daughter and son of two should be one of promise, decided she must abandon any hope of support from her husband. His brother and sisters came to her help by insisting that the house property be sold and the proceeds used to promote and equip a laundry business which Sarah would manage. Only one cottage was retained. When work began on it, John himself helped to build a long lean-to annex. He also agreed that his one remaining horse and cart should be used to carry the baskets of laundry. Large coppers were built and laundry equipment was installed: an enormous mangle and an ironing stove, together with long tables and great clothes' horses. Irons of various types also were obtained: flat irons, box irons, polishing irons with curved bases for starched shirt-fronts and goffering irons for frills and flounces.

Sarah set a high standard for her four or five laundry maids, and business came pouring in. Mrs Thomas Moy and Dr Witty were two Colchester customers. The Scriveners, Nicholls and Wilsons from the big houses of Ardleigh depended on Mrs Lewis to wash, starch and iron their linen. She and her children were well-known personalities, as they drove the horse and cart through country lanes delivering the large open-topped baskets covered with spotless blue-and-white cloths. On Saturdays, when the Colchester consignment was taken in, Sarah would return home with large quantities of soap, soda, bleaching-powder, starch and washing-blue.

It is a fantastic notion in the light of one's knowledge of modern London; but every Tuesday a large hamper of linen came from an Oxford Street store by rail to Ardleigh Station. It was laundered and returned on Friday. Only ten or fifteen years ago Sarah's daughter, then ninety, spoke of driving the cart to the station to collect it. She also told of a morning when she drove her father, resplendent in silk hat and flowered waistcoat, to the station to catch a train to London. The balance of the money from the sale of his property had been invested in Green and Bawtree's Bank, and John Lewis had been summoned to a meeting of creditors. He returned a broken man and, while his energetic little wife spiritedly carried on her business, became more and more morose. Known in the district as California Lewis or Foreigner Lewis, he did a little dealing in pigs and bought brandy casks to sell to farmers for feeding-troughs.

To provide fodder for his horse he would mow the wide by-road verges and take home the hay. In spite of his reputation for being at odds with life, he would willingly lend his horse and cart to anyone in the neighbourhood. That knowing animal frequently brought her master home without guidance. One night Sarah heard the pony return to the cottage, but John failed to appear. She began to be a little uneasy; but Lizzie Vaughan, her housekeeper, advised: 'Don't go to look for him; if he's fallen down the well you'll have to help him out.' So far had the once debonair sailor fallen in the estimation of acquaintances.

John died at the close of the century, and soon afterwards Sarah disposed of the business. The reputation of her laundry remained for a long time in the locality, and gentlemen shook their heads over their shirt-fronts, complaining that no one could launder like little Mrs Lewis.

(Winter 1965)

QUARRYMEN'S BARGAIN

Emyr Jones

In the vocabulary of the Welsh slate quarryman the term 'bargain' had a special meaning. It was the six yards or so of rock-face allocated to the 'crew' working on it in partnership. Long after most bargaining with management was being done with trade unions, each crew conducted their own at monthly meetings with the 'bargain-letter' at the rock-face.

Early in the morning of 'letting day' *(diwrnod gosod)* this quarry official started on his rounds, accompanied by the over-looker of the department. At each bargain their task was to decide on the quality and nature of the rock, and to fix accordingly the rate for every pound's worth of slate produced. If the rock was so hard or contained so much waste that, for instance, the crew could produce only £5 worth of slate during the month, the management

---

THE MILL

The high, square windows
have black stars in them
where glass has shattered.

Inside, charred beams and mossy
    stones.
Around the bare walls
that shiver with the hum of traffic.

I think I hear the looms,
chunk, shee . . . chunk, shee . . .

The clatter of wood and the whistles
of old men who sang and coughed
their busy lives away here.

Now there is a garden, wild,
but it has colours the workers
would have liked to cheer their eyes
as they turned from grafting
and met beauty with surprise.

Stephen Wade (Winter 1987)

A Lake District slate splitter. (D. J. Evans)

a ton for some time. The quarrymen's monthly 'waste account' *(cownt baw)* was made out on a separate slip and signed by the weigher, whose lot was not a happy one, because the figures were often hotly disputed.

In addition to producing slates and clearing waste, the quarrymen were able occasionally to include in their monthly bill one other item: 'levelling' *(codi bona)* at a rate of 7s. 8d. a square yard. They cut a straight base to the bargain, with a slight gradient to ease the task of pushing the heavy loads to the landing-plate or siding on their way to the waste-tip. Heated arguments often flared up between the crew and over-looker concerning the accuracy of his measurements and mathematics, and sometimes the men employed tricks to obtain the maximum reward for their labours. A favourite one was to conceal a few feet of tape in the hand.

For the first three weeks of the month the men were paid a basic minimum wage. Then, on the evening of 'big pay day' *(diwrnod tal mawr)*, a 'settling paper' was made out for each crew. At the top was shown the total sum due for slates, clearing waste and levelling, followed by various deductions for wages already paid, insurance, hospital fund contributions (voluntary) and such items as powder, rock drill at about 6d. a foot, iron and steel and sharpening of tools. A sample pay slip for a month in 1938 shows a total of £110 7s. 2d. and deductions of £47 13s. 2d. (wages £43 15s. 4d.). Out of the balance of £62 14s. the crew would probably have paid the odd £2 14s. to their young apprentice or journeyman for dressing the slates, and shared the rest equally among themselves.

On the evening of the 'big pay', after the sounding of the final hooter, one man from each crew proceeded to the main office and stood in the queue according to his number.

might agree to pay them 'poundage' amounting to £30, so that the wage bill would come to £35 for slates alone. Each crew had their own spokesman, and talented orators some of them were. Backed by occasional moans and grunts from the rest, they would complain of all kinds of handicaps and draw attention to the rapid deterioration of the rock. At this rate, they would argue, it would not be worth carrying their food to the quarry; only an increase of five or ten shillings in the pound would save them from the workhouse.

If this argument failed, another bargaining session began on the rate per ton for clearing rubble, which might consist of huge boulders to be broken down or of pieces small enough to be shovelled direct into the wagon. The rate for the job varied greatly over the years but remained at 18d.

Tray of money-tins, each numbered on the lid. (E. Emrys Jones)

The manager sat at a table covered with holed trays containing money-tins, as illustrated, each with the official number of the crew on the lid. He handed the tin through an open window, as the name and number were called by the chief clerk; and the crew's representative made a quick check to ensure that it was correct and according to the settling paper. He then tossed the empty tin into a huge open-mouthed sack hooked to the office wall and hurried off to a pre-arranged rendezvous. Each crew had its regular meeting place, which might have been any odd corner on the outskirts of the quarry. The journeyman was paid first so that he could go home, leaving the others to the highly confidential business of sharing out the money. Invariably the method was to deal it out pound by pound, like cards from a pack.

It was an age-old practice to conceal part of the big pay where the wife was not likely to find it. She knew the exact amount of the basic weekly wage but had little idea how much her husband received on big pay day. Of course, she could consult one of the other wives and compare wages, but it was useless to try to cross-examine any of her husband's partners. They knew that, if their secret leaked out, much harder and more serious bargaining would follow before peace was restored.

(Spring 1964)

SATURDAY CLOSING

Lettice Mawer

My grandfather owned a private bank in the High Street of the Wiltshire market town of Chippenham in the early years of the last century. During his regime there was a country-wide scare about the safety of private banks, and one Saturday he found a long queue, stretching in two directions, of customers waiting impatiently to withdraw their savings. Grandfather knew he had only to drive to London to get all the ready cash he needed, for his wife's father owned Parr's Bank, a large and wealthy concern. So the Chippenham clerks were told to be as slow as possible, to count each withdrawal twice over, to examine minutely each cheque presented and never to miss an excuse to come and consult Grandfather in his office. Towards midday the cash at the bank had dwindled perilously, so he bribed a man to climb to the top of the Town Hall and imperceptibly move the hands of the clock forward a few minutes. Twelve began to strike, the bank's doors were closed and Grandfather's honour was saved. He set out at once for London, and on Monday he reversed his orders, telling the clerks to pay every client as quickly as possible, for they had no doubt spent an anxious weekend. The building, with its fine balustrade, was later pulled down and re-erected in Kingswood with the name 'Chippenham Rooms'.

(Spring 1970)

A FEUD ON THE FARM

F. F. Nicholls

Arthur the wagoner and Bert the cowman were mates of mine some years ago on a large arable farm in Kent. Arthur had the traditional appearance of his trade: he was in his late sixties with rich red-brown face, large spreading, tobacco-stained moustache and a slow strength which still enabled him to walk about with a 2½-cwt sack of tick-beans on his back. He shared my grandfather's view that a good joke was a good joke for all time; thus he never heard a gun go off without remarking, "Nother empty bar'l an' Oi ain' 'ad a drop". He was a cheerful and confirmed atheist – an attitude which, in my experience, is surprisingly widespread among countrymen.

There was nothing whatever traditional about Bert's appearance. Though employed on a farm, he saw no more of the outside air than most factory workers; consequently he was sickly pale, and when he lifted the front of his flat cap his moist brown curls were seen flattened against the damp white skin. Yet he too was massively strong: he used to walk a large Shorthorn bull about like a poodle and carry a four-bushel sack of tail corn like a brief-

'Arthur was in his late sixties with a rich red-brown face, large spreading, tobacco-stained moustache and a slow strength . . .' (George Adamson)

case. He was a voluble teller of stories, all unprintable and nearly all about 'bits er sport' with girls at the Dreamland amusement park 'down Margit there'. Another favoured topic was his eccentric diet. 'Oi're a queer chap about moi grub, Fred,' he would say. 'Milk, milk, milk, all day in 'ere. When Oi git up 'ome Oi carn' stand the soight of it. Never 'ave n' butter on me bread, y'know. Jist a bit er jam, paste, all such as that.'

After I had been at the farm three weeks, the wagoner and I had taken our carts to the cowshed and were helping Bert to muck out. This was unusual, as Arthur was generally carting wurzels at that time of day. We went on working in utter silence, but that was quite normal on any farm; it was not until we had finished that Arthur spoke to me: 'Fred, ast 'im 'ow much straw 'e wants'.

I was astonished, for the two men were standing not more than 8 ft apart. 'How many bundles do you want today, Bert?' I asked, sensing a delicate situation.

'Couple er dozen,' said Bert, and stomped away to the dairy.

In the stable three hours later Arthur offered an explanation. 'Ole Bert's a funny chap, y'know,' he began, seating himself stiffly on the corn-bin. 'You 'ave to goo careful with 'im. Oi carn' make nothing of 'im meself. What! Oi could tell you a few things, on'y it ain' none o' moi business.' He paused, wondering which of the few things to tell me first. 'You know th'other day 'e took a bag o' tail corn over for 'is fowls? 'E wouldn' let you take it in the cart next day, same as you offered, would 'e? Well, did you know the ole chap [the farmer] was down town then? Oi ain' saying nothing, moind.' Another pause for thought. ''Nother thing: you know them 'utches where 'e gives out 'e's keeping rabbits?'

I said I did.

'Ferrets! Three-four of 'em. Out with 'em 'e is, pri-noigh every noight. You know Oi went acrost to Fettling Tuesday? Well, as Oi come back past the Wents, there 'e was with a pocketful o' rabbits. 'E went down quick in the doike, but Oi seen 'im alroight. Course, Oi don' say nothing. You know what, Fred? Pri-near makes me croy, the way 'e takes the ole chap in: yes

sir, no sir, three bags blooming full sir, to 'is face; then setting in that ole dairy rolling fags couple of hours a day an' putting in for everlasting of overtoime. You know that cow what went to the knacker's last week? All 'is fault, y'know. 'E made out there wadn' nothing wrong with 'er, till she doied. Then 'e up an' said 'twas the dusty 'ay Oi took acrost. No, Fred, 'e's a queer feller, an' Oi don' 'ave much to do with 'im. We don' know by roights where 'e come from, y'know. Down Margit way, 'e makes out, but Oi never 'eard of anyone what knew 'im out there. 'Owsumdever, there 'tis; you git some queer old turn-outs these days.'

As far as I was concerned Bert was friendly, cheerful and obliging. When we had finished in the cowshed of a morning he would usually squat back against a wall, as I

'There was nothing whatever traditional about Bert's appearance.' (George Adamson)

have seen miners do, saying, 'Well, 'ave a bit er shag now', and pulling out a tin and a packet of papers. Very often this little spell would be filled with unlikely adventures at Margate, but one day I managed to turn the conversation to the subject of Arthur and his family.

'Now there's a mean blooming crowd for you, Fred. Toight as a duck, they are, an' that's watertoight. Whoi, ole Arthur owes me pri-noigh seven-an'-six since last Christmas.'

'Perhaps there's some mistake?'

'Mistake? Ain' no blooming mistake about that, moi Fred. Jis' plain thieving, that's all. Oi give 'im ten bob of a Froiday to git me a 'alf-dollar postal order down town. 'E sent one of 'Orry's little ole boys acrost with it, an' Oi ain' seen moi blooming change yet, an' Oi lay Oi never shall now.'

'Have you ever asked him for it? He might easily have forgotten.'

A bitter snort. 'Oi ain' going to ast 'im for the blooming money; whoi don' 'e come acrost 'ere an' give it me? Oi don' want no favours off of 'im, not no charity. Course, y'know,' he went on, 'Oi ver'soon found 'im out, soon as Oi come 'ere from Margit: me an' 'im bought a cant er wood together in that old shaw 'soide moi 'ouse. Share an' share aloike, supposed to be. Silly-loike, Oi thought Oi'd 'ave enough foiring for all winter out er that. Well, you know what, Fred? Oi lay Oi never 'ad more'n a quarter er that wood. Noight after noight when Oi

was in 'ere milking, moi ole gal seen 'im goo by with a gurt old faggot on 'is back. Oi never bought n'more wood along of 'im.'

On another day the subject of straw led us to more of Arthur's failings. 'Well, Fred, Oi carn' 'elp about your raking, Oi shall 'ave to 'ave some more bundles acrost. Oi ain' got nowheres near enough as 'tis. Course, Oi don' say nothing, 'cause about you working with Arthur, but if we 'ad a couple er proper carts coming acrost with it, 'stead er that titchy ole thing 'e roides about on . . . What, Fred! Oi could git as much on the end er moi finger as what 'e gits in that cart. Oi lay when you first come 'ere 'e never give you the pick er them carts, did 'e? An' that 'orse of 'is ain' on'y 'alf the age er yourn, y'know. Course, it ain' nothing to do with me.' Then with another burst of indignation: 'See same as when you goo dung-cart, Fred, 'e ain' on'y got 'alf the load to what you got, to chuck up an' rake off, an' Oi lay 'e don' git done any quicker'n what you do. See Fred, 'e's 'aving you all ways. Oh, 'e's clever alroight: toidy soight cleverer 'n what Oi are.'

In the eight months that I knew them Arthur and Bert exchanged not a single word. The original quite small but real grievance between them had been built into a great thorny barrier of personal scorn and bitterness. The feud had in fact become a kind of family possession, a thing with a life of its own, which made a good sharp gritty corner in uneventful lives.   *(Spring 1963)*

TAIL CORN

Cheshire farm worker, of some rough weather that had blown away his garden shed: 'Ee, it were worse 'n a gale. It were one o' them theer torreadors'.   *(Spring 1958)*

The traveller. (J. F. Keene)

ODD JOBS, ODD FOLK

WITH COLD CASCADE

R. H. Wilson

Until 1905 the only fire engine in our Wiltshire village of Bishopstone bore the date 1690. There were no hoses, just a brass nozzle that could be swivelled through a comparatively small arc; and usually the water had to be carried to a canvas tank, as the suction pipe was only 16 ft long. There would be eight or ten pumpers and John Povey, the tailor, was captain of the team. He would stand on top of the engine, often perilously close to the fire because of the short range of the nozzle; but he enjoyed every minute of it, all the while puffing away at his huge pipe which he took out of his mouth occasionally to shout at some spectator to 'put that dam' pipe out'.

The *Swindon Advertiser* reported of a disastrous fire at Bishopstone church on Good Friday 1891: 'The old village fire engine was brought into requisition but proved to be of little use, not being powerful enough.' Nothing is known for certain of the engine's early history, but it probably belonged originally to Lord Holland; he owned most of the village in the seventeenth century when it was much larger than today and nearly all thatched. In the nineteenth century the engine must have passed into the hands of John Povey's grandfather and father who were the village constables, for it has been known as 'John Povey's engine' ever since. In 1905 John Whatley of Manor Farm, a wealthy eccentric, advanced £70 to the parish council to enable them to buy a secondhand Merryweather fire engine, and their seventeenth-century model passed eventually into the care of the Bath Central Fire Station where it can be seen today. John Povey's son Frank was the first captain to be in charge of the new engine.

Money had to be found to repay the advance, so neighbouring parish councils, from Uffington on the east to Wanborough on the west, were invited to pay a retaining fee of two guineas a year for the services of the Bishopstone brigade. Some, not surprisingly, declined to take advantage of the offer; we never saved anything more than a few tons of spoilt hay. Fortunately about three-quarters of our calls were to haystacks which, having started to burn from the centre by spontaneous combustion, could not have been saved anyway, even if we had been quicker on the scene.

There was one important fire at which we did turn up fairly promptly, the call having come just at closing time when all the firemen could be found in one place. There was an unwritten law – or so we imagined – that the captain first on the scene should take command of operations, even if two or three others arrived later. So, when a very efficient uniformed brigade with brass helmets and axes turned up from Stratton St Margaret, the two captains became engaged in bitter argument as to who should take precedence. Frank Povey was not the sort to yield, and the Stratton captain was equally determined not to place his *corps d'élite* under such a motley crowd as ours. To reach a compromise, he said, 'Well, we'll operate on the roof from the other side.' As soon as he had departed, Dobbin Durham spoke up: 'Now then, gi' I the nozzle, an' soon as 'e pokes 'is ruddy gurt 'ead over the top, arse over 'ead 'e goes.' In a matter of minutes we saw the captain's polished helmet appear over the roof, and as soon as his head and shoulders were in full view, Dobbin gave him the force of a jet provided by thirty-two willing pumpers, toppling him backwards like a sparrow.

On my return from the war in 1919 I found I had been appointed captain of the fire brigade in my absence. There was no telephone in the village, and our method of alarm was primitive in the extreme. At night I would be aroused by a stone thrown at my bedroom window, usually by a man on horseback. He would receive refreshment before returning to instil a little patience into those who had sent him. When I had dressed, I would hurry down to Jack Hunt, who provided the horses, and throw a stone at his window. If he had not too busy a day ahead of him, Jack would say, 'The 'osses is down in Latter Meadow, but I shan't be a jiffy.' Latter Meadow was a good three-quarters of a mile away, and the horses were always difficult to catch, especially in the dark; Jack also had to find two halters to lead them up. After making sure that he was taking matters seriously, I would chase round the village, bombarding the windows of the other members of the team, and telling them to hurry to the engine-house and get the doors unlocked. It was necessary to give this injunction to all, as no one knew who had the key; more often than not the lock had to be forced. I would then return to see how Jack Hunt was doing. It was not unusual to find him

having a cup of tea while the horses chewed at some oats and chaff in the manger. If I attempted to stress the urgency of the affair, he would say, 'I never reckons to take my 'osses out on an empty belly'.

Eventually we would be away on a journey of anything up to five or six miles, to find the fire well established. On arrival I had to issue my host of would-be pumpers (we required thirty-two – sixteen on each side) with arm bands, each with a numbered metal disc, and to enter their names with numbers in a book with the time of starting. While this formality was being performed, the fire looked after itself. I would be pestered by volunteers to 'go for the beer', it being generally accepted that this had priority over finding water, which was occasionally a great problem. I have often had 1,200 ft of hose in use for a haystack fire; but if someone could tell me exactly where water was and the best way to reach it, we could be in action in a very short time.

The greatest menace to property, next to the water we poured in, was the enthusiasm of the helpers. At my grandfather's home at Ashbury an old malt house had been converted to a study with two bedrooms; the upper storey was reached by an outside stone stairway. This building went up in flames one night, and volunteers swarmed over it immediately. As one carried a mattress down the stone steps, another struggled to the top with the piano and tipped it over the side. It exploded with a chord of music that echoed all round the village.

We did one fortunate and unusual piece of salvage at Wanborough. By this time I had a car of sorts and, having warned the team, I went ahead with two men to reconnoitre. Arriving at the scene about 3.30 a.m. we saw no sign of a conflagration; but a dim light in the kitchen window

Bishopstone fire brigade, 1905. (R. H. Wilson)

revealed the old farmer sitting by the fire with the teapot steaming at his side. Without rising from his chair he told me that, if I got on top of the hayrick just outside the door, I would find a hole about a yard square, reaching down to the ground, with a wet sack at the bottom, behind which I should find the fire. This I did, and the flames leapt out at me like an adder striking: the farmer had missed cutting into the furnace by about two inches. Hastily pushing the sack in again and pouring more water on it, I went up for air. If air were allowed to reach the fire, the whole stack would be in flames in seconds, and water would ruin the hay. But I told the farmer, who lived some way from the village, not to worry; I would save ninety-nine per cent.

By seven o'clock I had succeeded in borrowing four elevators, several hay knives and two or three helpers; and, starting at each corner, in the next few hours we built four 10-ton ricks of prime hay from one of 40 tons. When the original rick had been reduced to a cube of 2 ft and we could no longer avoid cutting through to the fire, we tidied up, removing any loose inflammable material. Then I pulled the sack out and there was a vivid flash of flame, which was reduced to a bucketful of ash in a few seconds. The insurance company were generous in the matter of beer and our charges.

After each fire it was my duty to submit our bill to the insurance companies, including those concerned with adjacent properties which had been in jeopardy. The problem was first to find out whether the

[41]

owners were insured; few of them knew, and policies were difficult to find, many being hopelessly out of date. What was more, no policy that I saw said anything about the company paying for the services of a fire brigade. Yet in all my twenty-two years as captain there was never an argument and seldom even a query. Our charges were as follows: captain, first hour 5s., subsequent hours 2s. 6d.; twelve firemen, 2s. 6d. and 1s. 6d.; thirty-two pumpers, 1s. 6d. and 1s. They were not pumping all the time, of course, but as long as they wore their arm bands they were entitled to the pay. When a farm worker's wage was 12s. a week, a 'good' fire, lasting two days or more, represented real wealth.

Payment was made to me personally, and then we had a share-out according to the time sheets I had compiled. I believe I was the only person in the village who realised that the insurance companies were under no obligation to pay; and I shudder to think what would have happened if I had not kept the knowledge to myself. The share-out was a red-letter day in the village, and between the end of a fire and the settling of the account I would be accosted a hundred times with, 'When be 'ee goin' to pay out for that fire at Smith's?' But one thing was to our credit: every single person in the village took an interest and pride in the fire engine. There was no quibbling or jealousy when the brigade members were selected.

Our quickest turn-out was in response to a false alarm, and on this occasion I nearly overdid it. Our nearest village, Bourton, had not accepted our offer of fire protection; but when a busy little retired Indian Army colonel came to live there and was made chairman of the parish council, the matter was raised again and they decided to put us on trial. It came to my ears that the colonel planned to arrange a bonfire of paper and empty boxes in his orchard, which was close to a pond, and then send for the Bishopstone Fire Brigade to put it out. Later I discovered the evening on which the scheme was to be carried out, and I cautiously warned all our members to rendezvous at a certain field about half way to Bourton, where Jack Hunt would have the engine ready limbered up behind a small copse. I was leaning over the gate smoking my pipe when a boy scout came cycling up the road from Bourton as if the devil were after him. 'What's the hurry, sonny?' I asked. 'Got to go to Bishopstone to fetch the fire brigade,' he yelled as he went round the corner. We galloped out of the gate like a half section of horse artillery and were on the scene before the colonel had got his bonfire going. While he was fumbling about with a match on one side, we gave it a terrific blast on the other, blowing his mountain of boxes and paper, still undamaged by fire or smoke, all over his orchard. This earned us Bourton's two-guinea retaining fee.

(Winter 1967)

A LEVEL LOST

An ear-muffed man
With his JCB
Came down for a week last year.
He dug the dykes
And he scoured the streams
In the course of his five-day week.
The water board pumped
And the farmers ploughed,
And the barley crop's been fine.
But the redshank's gone
And the snipe flew on;
The bladderwort's lost
And we're counting the cost
Of those extra tons of grain.

Norman Fryer (Spring 1984)

THE OLD TOFFEE-MAKER

Marjorie Giles

Old Toffee Tipton, who lived down the road, would be what is now called an anti-hero. Certainly his virtues were of a negative kind; he did not drink, he did not smoke and he was a mild-mannered little man. His shortcomings were too vague to be called vices; in fact, to most people he was just an ordinary chap. To us, the local children, he was rather special.

I am writing of the time around the beginning of the First World War which, living in a small country town in Shropshire, hardly affected us except that the world seemed a brighter place when our fathers came home on leave.

Toffee Tipton sold sweets. Not only did he sell them, but he actually made them, in a tiny one-man factory in the garden behind his little cottage. I had two brothers and two sisters (I was the girl in the middle) and to us getting into that factory was a step into another world.

Toffee Tipton was about seventy, a lean, shortish figure with a nut-cracker face, no teeth, sharp blue eyes, and a very pink skin. He had a sparse beard and snow-white hair. He always wore overalls and a flat tweed cap pulled down over his eyes. I never did see him without that cap. He was always busy and always worried. His wife and grown-up daughter both strongly disapproved of everything about him. Either of them had only to say 'Now, Father', in a warning tone, to send him scuttling down the brick path to his sugary sanctuary, inside which they never set foot.

The factory was built of brick, and from the outside it looked rather like a chapel, with narrow deep-set arched windows and a wide wooden door. Inside it was warm with the glow of the fire and fragrant with the aroma of peppermint, almonds, chocolate, and all sorts of mouth-watering smells. A huge brick stove with a blackened iron top stood at one end and on it several large pans bubbled away merrily.

Above the long table in the middle of the room two or three oil lamps were suspended from the crossbeam. On the table bowls, tins, spoons, bottles, scales and weights were spread in fascinating disarray. Along the walls were shelves filled with large jars of sweets, tins of toffee, stacks of paper bags, bottles of flavouring, and on the floor sacks of sugar with their tops turned back lolled against each other.

The most enchanting thing in the whole place was a machine which, when Toffee Tipton turned a handle, set in motion four metal arms which, passing through a bowl of soft toffee, turned and twisted and stretched it over and over again until it was of the right texture. The old man would pull out a piece of toffee about 6 in. wide and a yard long, and cut it off with an enormous pair of scissors; then he put it in another machine – a cross between a mangle and a mincer – turned a handle, and a shower of caramels would fall into the bowl beneath.

If one of us had a penny or even a halfpenny to spend, we could all go in through the gate and down to the factory. Once inside, Toffee Tipton would let us stand by the door, watching, for as long as we liked, but if we forgot and crept nearer, he would be afraid of our being splashed with boiling sugar. Then he would shout, 'You – you – you kids get outa here. I wunna have ye meithering me.' Then he

'On the table, bowls, tins, spoons, bottles, scales and weights were spread in fascinating disarray.' (Brian Walker)

would push a handful of sweets into our fists and scowl, with a twinkle in his eye, 'Now get off with ye'. He never accepted our pennies.

On one never-to-be-forgotten occasion, when I was the only spectator, Toffee Tipton actually asked if I would like to oil the moulds for the sugar mice. I was delighted. There were two dozen moulds in trays of six, rather similar to mother's buntins. I had a little brush, and some olive oil in an old cup, and my job was to see that each mould was given a very thin coating of oil. Then Mr Tipton came and poured the shining, almost transparent syrup into each mould. As it cooled, it became hard and opaque and, when about half set, we poked string tails dipped in sugar syrup into each mouse. Later on, when they were turned out, Mr Tipton gave them pink cochineal eyes and noses. That was a great day.

We used to like watching the humbugs being made. Two slabs of soft, peppermint-flavoured toffee, one black, one white, were put together and worked by hand, folding and stretching over and over again, until the two intermingled in black and white stripes. The stripes got narrower with each folding until at last the toffee was ready to go through the cutting machine.

Sometimes, if the old man was not quick enough with the folding, the toffee would set hard, and then it would not go through the machine. Then it would be left in slabs, broken up with a toffee hammer, and sold in lumps. These lumps had very sharp corners but they lasted a long time, and so were very popular with us.

Often, of course, we did not have any money to spend. Then we did not dare pass Mrs Tipton's door; she was quite likely to pop out and demand evidence that we were bona-fide customers. We had a routine approach to this problem. We would gather together, and casually mention to mother that we were going to play in the old pig-sty at the bottom of the garden. Well, so we

did, but not for long. Soon we would decide to 'go trailing'.

Although we girls knew that we should be scolded for such unlady-like activities, the temptation was strong, and more often than not we followed where the boys went, hoping we might get away without tearing our rather bulky clothing. My elder brother always went first, and he led us through a hole in the hedge, then on all fours past the currant bushes in the next-door garden, and into the hen-run. Very quietly, so as not to start the hens squawking, we climbed on top of the pen, over the wire and into the over-hanging branches of the apple tree behind the factory, down on to the grass and finally, with great caution,

'Very attractive it looked with boxes and jars of humbugs caramels, pearldrops, Turkish delight . . .' (Brian Walker)

round the corner of the fuel shed and in through the door, without falling foul of Mrs Tipton.

On Wednesdays and Saturdays Toffee Tipton used to get out his old handcart from the shed, dust it down, and load it up with his wares, adding a pair of shiny brass scales and weights, a selection of paper bags and an Oxo tin containing a shilling or two in coppers. Then he pushed it down to the market and set up his stall under the Butter Cross along with all the country folk who had brought in their farm produce.

Very attractive it looked with boxes and jars of humbugs, caramels, peardrops, Turkish delight, pipes and boot-laces of liquorice, aniseed balls, treacle toffee, bull's eyes, gobstoppers, sugar-mice and sugar-pigs with curly string tails, and pretty little scented sweets in delicate colours of mauve, white, pink, green and yellow, which looked like little satin cushions. In those days you got a lot for a penny!

One Wednesday morning, just as Mr Tipton was setting up his stall, he saw the young squire coming along in his new motor car; at that time still a novelty. The noise of the car frightened a pony being driven by a farmer; the pony reared and the farmer's wife was thrown out of the trap.

Toffee Tipton fortunately managed to catch her or she would have crashed into one of the stone pillars of the Butter Cross. Both he and the farmer's wife fell on the sharp cobblestones; she picked herself up and ran after her husband without a word of thanks to poor old Toffee, who himself was suffering from several cuts and bruises. His stall had been overturned by the plunging pony, and all his goods trampled into the ground; quite a heavy loss for him. However, he told my father some time later that when the old squire heard of the incident he made ample recompense.

After the war we moved to another part of the county, and later I heard that my old friend had died. Most of his sweets were priced at a penny for a quarter of a pound, so Toffee Tipton could never have made much money. He would have found the changing world difficult, and a modern public health officer would give his little factory short shrift, with its lack of fire precautions and unhygienic conditions. But I never heard of anyone taking harm from eating Toffee Tipton's sweets.

(Summer 1971)

MAN OF PARTS

Nancy Mercer

He was our village odd-job man, and there cannot be many like him to-day. A chauffeur-valet, he could also lay out a garden, do topiary and greenhouse work, pick and market fruit and vegetables, graft apples and plums, and bud roses. He did decorating and plumbing, repaired cars, motor cycles, bicycles, tractors and other farm implements and soldered milk buckets and urns: he could thatch a rick or a house, mend a gate, lay a hedge and milk a cow. During the war years he cut down old trees and sawed them up, but always planted new ones in their places; at this time, too, he was a special constable. When required he would sole and heel shoes, upholster a suite of furniture, repair clocks and watches and spectacle frames, put new glass in windows or a grate in a room, or sweep a chimney. He would shave any sick man in the village and cut his hair, and would sit up all night with a sick animal. He was a bell-ringer, acted as sexton and grave-digger if no one else was available, sang in the church choir and also at concerts, played the banjo and the bones. He could do fretwork well. At evenings and weekends he cultivated his own three-quarters of an acre of garden, growing fruit, vegetables and flowers and keeping fowls: he had a good knowledge of herbs and knew how to make wines at home: he was a good cook and could take over other household duties when his wife was ill. He had wonderful patience and did everything extremely well. He was my father.

(Winter 1968)

BAT-FOWLERS

Charles Gardiner

I remember the bat-fowlers who worked the hedges at night to capture small birds. The dressing of them was a tedious business, but in a pie they made a welcome addition to cottage fare before the 1914–18 war.

In a Worcestershire village a party of six went bat-fowling regularly, their favourite hunting ground being a hedge running up the steep hillside behind the village. Amos would work up one side, beating with his stick. On the other, four men in pairs held two long poles with a net stretched between them high against the hedge. As the small birds flew out into the mesh, the poles were quickly brought together to trap them. Supervising the operation was Fred, who carried the lantern. There was no natural gap nor even a field gate throughout the whole length of the thick overgrown hedge, so Amos met the rest of the party at the top of the hill. Then, after examining the bag by the light of the lantern, they made their way down to the Green Dragon for pints of cider.

One night Fred and his companions decided to play a trick on their beater. As Amos whacked the hedge lustily, they folded their nets and stole away. He arrived at the top of the hill to find nobody to greet him, and soon realised what had occurred. But when eventually he joined the others in the Green Dragon, he seemed to take it all in good part.

The following Thursday the party were making their way along the hedge as usual when, half way up, Fred and his assistants heard a heavy splash followed by the thrashing of water and loud cries from Amos. Then came ominous gurgling noises, which suddenly ceased. All was still. Fred sent two men quickly round the top of the hedge and, with the others, raced round the bottom to a pond on the far side. When they met by the dark shining water, the surface was still faintly disturbed. Even on a summer's day the pond had a sinister air, and it could be deep after heavy rains. They stood in silence at first; then Fred's far-carrying voice rang out: 'Amos, Amos,

ABOVE: *'Amos, Amos, where are you?'* (Brian Walker)

BELOW: *'Will you please come in, Fred?'* (Brian Walker)

where are you? Where've you got to?' All they heard in reply was the hoot of a distant owl and the sound of a rabbit scuttering in the nearby undergrowth. As the beam of the lantern roved the pond, Fred saw something which left him in no doubt: Amos's cap lay near the edge.

Slowly and sadly the party moved down the hill, until Fred suddenly put a question which made them stop in their tracks: 'Who's going to tell his old mam?' He found himself saddled with the painful duty. Left a widow with a young family, Martha Brown had grown sharp of tongue and countenance, so that she was considered a bit of a terror by the younger men in the village. She had in her eldest son Amos a prop who helped to sustain the family and avoid the need to seek poor relief, dispensed with a niggardly hand by the board of guardians.

Fred's companions stood in a group under a tree across the way as, with some trepidation, he knocked at Martha's door. She recognised him at once, and, if she was surprised to see him, she gave no sign of it. 'Will you please come in, Fred?' she said. He stepped into the living-room which was lighted by an oil lamp on the table. Martha closed the door. 'Well?' she inquired as she faced him.

Fred twisted his cap nervously. 'It's about Amos,' he said.

'Well, what of 'im?' his mother demanded.

'You see, missus, 'e's gone. That's the trouble. Poor Amos be gone.'

'Of course, 'e's gone,' she snapped. ''E's been gone this ten minutes – soon as 'e finished 'is supper. You'll find 'im down at the Dragon. Got 'is best Sunday cap on.' And she became thoughtful as she said to herself: 'I 'ope 'e 'an't started a-courtin'.'

At this point Fred decided to retire quietly and in good order.

(Winter 1964)

SHE WAS AN ADMIRAL'S DAUGHTER

Maurice Broadbent

The old boatman told me this story as I sat beside him on a barrel, waiting for his son Jack to bring his boat back from a trip to the Bishop's Rock. He pointed to some chimneys showing above distant trees:

'Ole Miss Trezize use t' live up top the 'ill in the white 'ouse there. Admiral's daughter 'er was, an' as stately an ole figure'ead as you ever see. I've 'eard tell as 'er was a bit short with 'em in the shops if they didn't 'ave zackly what 'er wanted, but 'er was always all right to me an' Boy Jack. Took a walk along the front every mornin' 'er did, 'er an' 'er little dogs, an' then down to the 'arbour wall, use t' lean over an' say "Mornin', Mr Mynheer, mornin', Boy Jack", an' 'er would ask 'ow the sea was an' 'ow we expected to do. An' 'twadn' no use tellin' 'er the sort o' yarn us tells the visitors. 'Er knew the name of every rope an' every bit o' tackle, an' so 'er should, 'cause 'er was a Admiral's daughter. Then one day 'er didn' come, so I said to Boy Jack that per'aps 'er'd gone off up the county to see a relation.

'Mornin', Mr Mynheer, mornin', Boy Jack.' (Anne E. Hodgkiss)

'Bout a week later us was paintin' the boat up a bit when I looked up the 'ill an' see this 'ere foreigner chap comin' down. Bowler 'at 'a 'ad, an' a long face to 'en. 'A come down to the wall an' 'a says, "Can you tell me where I can find a man 'oo do own a boat 'ereabouts, called Mynheer? I've got a message fer 'en," 'a says, "from Miss Trezize". "Oh," I says, "in that case ye're talkin' to 'en now. What do the ole gel want?"

"Well, I'm sorry to tell 'ee as 'ow 'er's dead," 'a says, an' 'a went on as 'ow 'a was 'er lawyer an' 'ow 'er will asked that 'er should be buried at sea without any fuss. An' the ole gel 'ad 'ad it put down in writin' that 'er wanted me an' Boy Jack to do the job in my boat. I says 'twas right an' proper what 'er wanted done, 'cause 'er was a Admiral's daughter. "You 'ave the ole gel down 'ere Wednesday," I says, "an' us'll do the job fer 'ee."

Wednesday come, an' I 'ad me best 'at on, an' Boy Jack 'ad gone an' bought one special. Us 'ad the ole boat all done up, 'ad a bit o' black round the rowlocks an' all. 'Bout eleven o'clock this little percession come down the 'ill, with the ole gel on a trolley an' the vicar in that white thing 'a do wear Sundays, an' last the lawyer chap from Plymouth with a top 'at on. "'Ow much lead 'ave 'ee got in there, then?" says I to 'en, pointin' to the ole gel's box. "'Bout thirty pound," 'a says. "'Ow, don' 'ee think that'll be nuff?" "Maybe 'a is an' maybe 'a idn'," I says. "Any'ow, less 'ave the ole gel down in the boat."

Boy Jack took off 'is 'at an' I took off mine, 'cause 'er was a Admiral's daughter, see, an' us started to row out. Well, 'e wadn' zackly what I'd call rough, nor 'e wadn' zackly what I'd call smooth; 'e was just a bit pitchy like. I says as 'ow I was sorry to be doin' this for the ole gel, 'cause 'er 'ad always been all right to us. "But I'm not takin' anythin' fer this," I says. "I'm goin' to do this fer nothin', 'cause 'er was a Admiral's daughter." That there lawyer chap, 'a never said a word, 'a was too busy 'angin' on.

Us'd got a good way out when Vicar 'gun to get all worried up 'bout the three-mile limit. "Got to bury 'er out beyond that," 'a says, "'e's the law." "An' d'you know where that d' be, Vicar?" I says to 'en, "'cause I can tell you there's no line marked on the water." Then the lawyer chap come out with the tale that when you couldn't see ole Bishop's 'Ead any more that was about it. 'Nother 'alf an hour or so an' 'a says it's all right. So us gets the ole gel up over the side, an' Vicar gets 'e's book out an' d' say a prayer er two. "An' the body shall be cast into the sea," 'a says, an' us ler 'er go.

Sink? 'Er never thought any more 'bout it. The minute us let 'er go, 'er was off like a motor-boat. Goin' like a rocket 'er was, fer the shore. I 'ollered to Boy Jack, "Take 'old the oars, boy, an' after 'er, else she'll be back in the 'arbour afore we!" Boy Jack rowed an' I stood up in the prow with a boat'ook. Us 'd just caught up with 'er an' I was goin' to lay to 'er with the boat'ook when 'er up on end an' went down fer the last time. "God rest 'er soul," says the lawyer chap, an' Vicar 'a says "Amen".

Us turned round then 'an put back towards the bay. Vicar wadn' lookin' very 'andsome, an' the lawyer were a bit green. 'A'd lost 'e's top 'at somewhere, an' Vicar 'ad got 'e's ole white thing all wet. Well, 'e wadn' zackly what I'd call rough, an' 'e wadn' zackly what I'd call smooth; 'e was pitchin' a fair bit. Us 'adn't got more 'n back into view 'o the ole Bishop's 'Ead when the lawyer chap was took bad an' leaned over the side, an' Vicar was watchin' 'en an' all of a sudden 'a joined the lawyer. So I says to Boy Jack, "Lay 'old the oars, boy, an' put about. Us've got 'nother couple o' jobs on our 'ands!"

There you are, sir, there's Boy Jack comin' back in. If you go down the steps you'll just catch 'en. 'Tis the blue boat, only 'er's got a engine now, an' 'er name's painted on that white panel. You'll like 'er name, sir: 'tis "The Admiral's Daughter".'

(Autumn 1963)

SORCERER'S APPRENTICE

Moya Dewar

My father made medicines, ointments and pills from the herbs gathered as he roamed the countryside on his ancient bicycle. As soon as I was of an age to distinguish a dandelion from a buttercup he commenced my initiation. I was very conscious of my importance as part of the mystery; it put me one up on my friends.

We lived in a small old-fashioned town with a bi-weekly market where itinerant vendors of herbs and medicines would sometimes set up a stall. They were wonderful entertainers and first-rate psychologists. In the trade they were known as 'crocuses'. They would launch into their patter, frighten the lives out of their audiences with horrifying details of the diseases that awaited them and then, as the symptoms began to manifest themselves, move in with their cures at a shilling a bottle. Sales were usually pretty brisk in those pre-National Health days. They had their gimmicks too. One always kept his herb-gathering hand gloved – to maintain its purity, he said. Another drew his crowd by waving a flashing sword round his head and then neatly splitting a potato held on the outstretched hand of a local volunteer.

Part of my job as sorcerer's apprentice was to keep an eye on the crocuses and report to my father any new arrival. I would wriggle my way to the front of the crowd, note what was being sold and the manner of selling, and try to estimate how much money was taken at each session. It was a fascinating job. By the time I was ten I had a good working knowledge of the human anatomy and a stock of coarse stories that would have astounded a navvy. Most of the crocuses did a one-night stand and were not seen again, but if any looked like making our town a regular port of call, Father would investigate personally. If they were genuine he would leave them alone, unless they happened to have some remedy he had not yet come across, when he would hound them until they parted with their secret. He was very overpowering. I remember an insurance agent once calling to sell us a policy and leaving fifteen minutes later with a dazed look and a bottle of blood tonic. Being a bit of a rogue himself, Father was quick to detect signs of chicanery in others. When he made up his mind to drive a crocus off his stamping ground it was sure to be a battle royal.

There were two fellows I especially remember. One called himself a gypsy and went under a famous Romany name. He ran for about three weeks before Father decided his hour had come. The gypsy was offering a bottle of medicine positively guaranteed to cure gall-stones, kidney trouble, disturbed nights and cirrhosis of the liver. He named all the herbs that had gone into the making of this mixture, with lurid stories of the rites of gathering them. How often I heard about the mandrake that shrieked in agony as its roots were pulled up! Then came a bull-like roar from Father, and he slapped his thigh triumphantly. The gypsy had mentioned among his ingredients two herbs whose actions were diametrically opposed; one was a laxative, the other a specific for tightening up the bowels. I never heard Father in finer form than on that day. By the time he had finished enlarging on the state of the human gut after these two herbs had worked their stop-go action, the audience was in stitches and the gypsy choking with rage. He left and we never saw him again.

The other fellow lasted a little longer – about a month, I think – and this time I was brought in to help. He was clever, he seemed genuine, his patter was faultless and Father had not been able to catch him out. He was doing well too. We saw people returning for more boxes of pills, and yet Father's nose was twitching: the unmistakable smell of trickery was there. When we spotted an old woman who had bought Father's embrocation for years handing over her shilling for pills, he knew the time had come for desperate measures. He bought a box of pills himself and took them home for investigation. They were pure soap with a coloured sugar coating.

Next market day we waited behind the obelisk till our crocus had gathered a sizeable crowd and then we moved in,

'The audience was in stitches and the gypsy choking with rage.' (Brian Walker)

Father with his shilling to buy more pills, and myself well hidden behind him with a bottle of water, basin and clay pipe. When the man had finished and people were just going to step up for their pills, Father gave his usual bellow, which stopped them in their tracks. Then with a grandiose bow to the crocus he handed over his shilling, took a box of pills and tipped them into the bottle of water I handed to him. This he shook violently before pouring the contents into the white basin which I was holding out like an acolyte. He hoisted me on to the stall and, trembling with excitement, I dipped my little clay pipe into the mixture and blew a gorgeous fat iridescent bubble. It floated lazily above the crowd and headed for the Town Hall.

There was a dead silence as all heads turned to follow the progress of the soap-bubble. The crocus stood with a look of stupefied cunning on his face, his hands full of pillboxes. Father broke the silence with another roar, 'Yah, soapy pills! Soapy pills!' I blew bubbles like a thing possessed. Some burst in my face, children jumped round trying to catch them, the mixture slopped down the front of my dress, there was laughter and catcalling, and above all Father's voice bellowing 'So-o-apy pills!' The pandemonium brought the market inspector at a scurry, and a three-cornered argument ensued. I continued blowing bubbles: the wonder was that there could be so many. Doubtless the few soap-flakes Father had put in the bottle helped.

The fun came to an end at last and we marched off in triumph, half the crowd following us. My clay pipe was dropped and trodden on, but what a fortune in pennies I collected! Looking back I caught the eye of the discomfited quack. He shrugged opened his case and started packing.

(Winter 1962)

PROFESSOR HAMELIN

Edgar Hadley

He came one Saturday afternoon when the family were away and I was collecting tools and courage to paint the kitchen. With his thick, curly, brown hair, weather-beaten face and long, brown overcoat, he reminded me a little of the only professor who had ever given me alpha for an essay. In this part of the world we know these men by their overcoats and the testimonials they fish up from within. They come with ancient lorries or Heath Robinson cars to sell us manure, or buy our holly or cupressus clippings or old iron. The overcoats, always long, and whiskery at the cuffs and skirt, are worn all the year round. The testimonials, now creased and dirty, have to be unfolded with care if they are not to fall to pieces.

'Come to rid you of your rats and moles, Guv,' said the Professor, as if he had arrived by arrangement with the local council. 'Finish 'em off now or they'll only get worse. Multiply they do, something terrible. I don't use no traps nor no poisoned baits. I stops up the 'oles and gives 'em gas. One whiff and they're dead. Just like that.'

My mention of our terrier and rat-catching cat was brushed aside. 'Look here, Guv, I'm an old hand at this game.' One hand dived inside his coat and pulled out the inevitable paper headed 'To Whom It May Concern' and a faded brown photograph showing a younger edition of himself standing beside a revolting pile of dead rats. 'See what I mean?' he demanded. 'Now let's go down and look at your hen run and I'll tell you what I'll do.'

Whether it is the pathetic bits of paper, the shabbiness of the dreadful coats or the mesmeric assumption of confident authority I am never sure; but at the time it is always easier to be a sucker and say 'Uh-huh' than to be tough and say 'No'. Down in the hen run the Professor planned his attack. He would stop up all the holes save one and pump his gas down that. It was the last job of the day, so he would do it cheap: ten bob's worth of chemicals and ten bob for the job. 'Clear you of rats for a year for a quid, Guv.' I loathe rats. I also loathe putting down poison. Perhaps this one-whiff business would make a more merciful riddance.

By the time I left him to assemble his

gear and returned to the kitchen the kettle was whistling its spout off and I remembered I had been going to make tea. It would have been churlish not to offer Professor Hamelin a cup. Yes, he would like one. Sugar? 'If it's not robbing you, Guv.' When he finally returned to the garden, a long metal cylinder slung from one shoulder by a leather strap, he walked with a swagger that was plain invitation; so after a while I followed him. The hens were huddled in the farthest corner of the run, the overcoat was hanging from one corner of the hen-house, and the Professor was at the pump. At every thrust of the plunger a little white cloud came from the bottom of the cylinder. 'Leaking a bit', he said cheerfully; but he was quite certain that in the open air it would not hurt the hens: 'Splash a bit of water round, and Bob's your uncle.'

Hearing that rats also enjoyed the hospitality of the compost heap outside the run, he moved his contraption and pumped his witch's brew into that too. He cocked an ear over the heap, listening for last words from the inmates. 'I'll wager there ain't one alive. Won't see no more of 'em for a year at least. Now what about moles?' He looked hopefully round. 'I can rid you of moles for five years. Moles bothering you, Guv?' 'No,' I said, this time quite firmly, and moved between him and the potato patch, where the dog was scrabbling at a newly raised tump.

Back at the house I provided a pail of hot water and some soap, and he washed his hands with great care. 'Don't do to take no risks,' he said. 'This stuff's so strong that, if you had a dog with mange or distemper you wanted ridding of, just one sniff and he'd be on his back. Much quicker than anything a vet can do.' But the distant whimpers of excitement suggested neither disease; so when he had packed up his gear and donned his coat he climbed into his car, and I went into the lane to signal him out. As he drove off he waved goodbye with my beautiful pound and called, 'Back next week, Guv', whether to collect the corpses or as a pledge of good faith was not clear.

That evening, when I went to close the hen-house pop-hole, two grey shadows were draped over the farther feeding trough. As my hand went up to the gate latch they slid back to the ground, and the next moment they were swallowed up in the blackness of the open hole. Perhaps they were only ghosts, or perhaps someone had put in a snappy bit of reincarnation; but by next morning the feeding troughs had been polished as clean as ever and at least three holes reopened.

That was a month ago. There has been no sign of the ancient car or its driver down our lane since, and I can be certain only that I have got rid of Professor Hamelin and a pound note.

(Summer 1958)

A CHANGE OF HOME

Dominic Reeve

It was Sunday afternoon, so nobody was working. The sun shone brightly with the unwearying heat of early summer.

There were twenty-four horse-drawn vans, a few square-framed and 'bender' tents and four modern trailer caravans drawn by lorries round the edges of the field which the farmer had set aside for travellers during the pea-picking. As the afternoon wore on, several more lorries and motor-vans arrived with travellers of all ages visiting friends and relatives. The drivers negotiated the hundred yards or so of rough pot-holed track from the highway to the field with complete disregard for the springs of their vehicles. So each arrived with the occupants tousled, out of breath, laughing and shouting, disarrayed after having been tossed like stones in a can.

Just at that time Beshlie and I had a little light-weight 'open-lot' wagon with canvas top and wood back and front. It had been built up on a flat trolley by an amateur carpenter for the traveller from whom we had acquired it two months earlier. It was not a good wagon; being top-heavy it was apt to sway in a wind, like a full-rigged ship in a storm. In a gale it would be overturned if not pegged down. But wagons of any sort are scarce nowadays, and I had had to buy it, having sold our previous one to a non-traveller for a fancy price (one can never afford to turn away a good deal, nor does one wish to do so); it was the only wagon 'for trade' in the area in which we were then travelling. It cost £10 and was very rough: grass had been growing inside under the bed, and the canvas top had leaked badly. But after the interior had been relined with bright fabric and the canvas roof and sides given a coat of proofing, it had become a moderately attractive little home.

Ever since our arrival three days earlier I had noticed, though only from his eyes, that Little Jesse was interested in our wagon. His was much larger than ours and was too heavy for his pony, being barrel-topped with over-solid underworks. Its canvas sheet was in no better condition than our own, but the shape and original workmanship were good. We talked to-

gether about it and decided that it had possibilities. At least it had been built as a wagon and was not, like most of the others (ours included), merely a built-up trolley. It also had a considerable amount of scalloping and decorative work which could be picked out in contrasting colours. At the time it was dark crimson with yellow underworks, and unavoidably smoke-dulled by the outside fires which invariably cover everything and everyone in soot.

Sunday is always regarded as a good day for dealing. Two wagons had already changed hands, and Sleepy Joe had bought a nice tight little cob from Eli's Jim. So it was no great surprise when Jesse casually wandered over to our fire with his small son, lay down traveller-style, his body propped on one elbow, and started to smoke a thin hand-rolled cigarette. His handsome angular dark features were creased by lines so deep that his mouth and nose seemed secondary in importance to them. His piercing eyes glittered from under the brim of his old cap. He wore faded green corduroy trousers made 'Ockford fashion' with fall-fronts, aged brown boots and an oversize blue lounge-suit coat. A bright silk scarf was knotted crosswise at his neck in the formal style of London costermongers of old. This has now been widely adopted by the travellers who still wear scarves, in preference to the more old-fashioned method of merely winding the handkerchief twice round the neck and knotting the ends, which were left loose or might sometimes be tied in a bow.

We had just made some tea, so we gave Jesse a cup. Sure enough he gradually turned the conversation round to the subject of wagons, and his own in particular. 'Had un off some London travellers,' he declared, pausing for effect. (London travellers have always been held in great respect by down-country people and as-

'We had just made some tea, so we gave Jesse a cup.' (Brian Walker)

sumed to have superior horses and equipages.) After looking round the meadow with some distaste, he went on: 'Ain't n'arn a wagon in this field as is better 'n mine. Fact the matter is mine's the bestest-made wagon fer fifty mile or more – not that I'm proud, mind, an' I ain't particular about gettin' rid of un. But like me poor dead father allus said, "A good thing'll sell itself; 'tis on'y rubbish needs pushin'"'.'

"Tisn't a bad ole wagon,' I agreed without enthusiasm. If it had been the best I had

ever seen I would naturally not have divulged the fact by any outward sign. Hard times leave such legacies.

'Go an' have a look at it, *mush*, if you like. Don't be ashamed. Go up into it. Go where you likes. You couldn't fault it, 'ceptin' he needs a coat o' paint, o' course, but that wouldn't take hardly a minute. I'd do it meself if I had the time, though I ain't much of an oil-painter, mind.' I merely glanced in the direction of his wagon and nodded.

By this time, sensing that a deal might be

imminent, several other men had sauntered up to our fire. A traveller's life is not private, and everyone likes to watch a transaction; much face is lost or gained by a deal, and a man is given a chance to show himself to advantage or otherwise.

I looked towards our wagon, shuddered inwardly at its ugliness and began to extol its virtues in as colourful and exaggerated a manner as I could, laying especial emphasis on its lightness, with Jesse's small pony in mind. I knew that he would sooner change his wagon than part with that pony. Rather than sell it or 'chop it away' he would try to get our small wagon. I also knew that he had not money enough to buy a second, larger cob outright at that time; and by the way the pea-picking was going it did not seem likely that he would have much more at the end of it, particularly as he did not have a large family to work with him and jump up his earnings. ' . . . Everything shall be right and sound. And that wagon so clean that you could eat your food off the floor; in fact I have done it,' I terminated quite breathless with enthusiasm for the well-hidden qualities of the wagon.

Several of the other travellers smiled but, quite rightly, Little Jesse appeared as unimpressed by my oration as I by his. He puffed his cigarette and said nothing. I lit one myself with a brand from the fire and sat staring silently into it.

'Come on you two, is you goin' to have any trade or not?' shouted Diddler from the next fire, twenty feet away.

'Goo on, try to have a deal! Let's see some o' they ole green pound notes flyin' about,' called Old Siddy hoarsely. He had not tired of seeing deals, though he was over eighty.

An Elvis Presley record blared incongruously from a portable gramophone beside Henry's wagon a hundred feet away. ' . . . Ah'm all shook up! Yeah, ah'm all shook up!' The metallic, fascinatingly garish music clanged and boomed; and several of the younger youths became infected by it and gave impromptu demonstrations of abandoned rock 'n' roll gyrations to the great delight of those near them.

Jesse looked hard at me for a moment, then commenced the deal in earnest. 'How much will you gie me to chop wagons, *mush?*' he asked quickly.

'Me! Oh, my poor dead grandmother!' I retorted, firing straight back. 'Gie me twenty pounds and I'll chop. My wagon cost me all of eighty pounds.'

'What! Mine cost me a hundred. Twenty pounds to chop, not today, brother,' exclaimed Jesse, his face assuming an expression of outraged indignation.

The record changed, and casual relaxing strains wafted towards us as we became more tense: 'Soon I'm goin' to see that love-look in her eyes . . .' The music swept over and around us.

'Goo on, ask him sensible; try an' have a deal,' shouted one of the onlookers.

'Goo on, Jesse! Make him a bid!'

The relaxed, vaguely sensual voice of the young singer drowned and swamped us, to be violently interrupted every few seconds by a hoarse cry from a spectator or a shouted offer from either Jesse or myself.

The deal progressed gradually, for more than an hour had passed with Jesse coming up from his starting point and me coming down; as he was the bidder and instigator of the deal it was bound to take that form. Only a pound separated us between Jesse's bid and my asking price for a 'chop'. The hard faces all round us were tense and excited, waiting for the conclusion. The music had been stopped. Both Jesse and I were weakened with exertion and overstimulated emotions. The energy and vigour which must be thrown into a travellers' deal is quite phenomenal, and the climax is aesthetic. Whenever I buy from or sell to a non-traveller I am always sensible of a lack of enjoyment; then everything is brought down to a mundane and rather depressing level.

'I'll gie you nine pounds to chop, *mush*, I'll gie you nine pounds to chop,' urged Jesse.

'Goo on, *mush*, don't let a pound note part you. Try to make a deal. Goo on.'

'Gie me ten pounds to chop 'an not a penny less,' I shouted back.

Jesse suddenly went very quiet, and I knew the climax was near. He stood up, walked towards me and stretched out a hand to grip mine and hold it palm upper-most; then he raised his other hand to strike my open palm and settle the deal in the traditional way. He spoke quite softly: 'Now brother, if you wants to make a deal here's me very last bid. An' if it ain't, then may I never see me dear mother alive no more, an' may me baby die if I bids another ha'penny arter this.' He paused a moment for effect and continued: 'I shall gie you nine pound notes an' half a sovereign. An' if I does that, will you gie me back two half-crowns fer luck, or won't you? Yes or no. Quick.'

I looked him in the eye for a moment; then I held out my hand and his palm struck mine. The deal was done. The onlookers breathed again and a flood of talk broke

'The deal was done.' (Brian Walker)

loose. Little Jesse called to his wife to bring the money, for travelling women usually look after that, in case the men spend it too freely when under the influence of drink or out of bravado. He counted out the notes singly and slowly into my hand; and I returned him two halfcrowns for the tradi-tional luck money. That night Beshlie and I slept in yet another wagon; it was our thirty-second.

(Spring 1960)

A PROPER JOB

L. G. Taylor

I bumped into Charlie one evening when he was on his way home from milking. 'Jus' the man,' he said. 'My missus do want the kitchen done out. Would 'ee mind lookin' in at un one night?'

I do a bit of decorating as a side line, just

to oblige, as the saying is, and I looked in a couple of evenings later to size up the job. Charlie, I discovered, had a passion for pin-ups; anything from a beauty queen to the State Opening of Parliament. The kitchen, where he and his wife did everything was the picture-gallery of a lifetime's collecting.

It was too late to back out. With Charlie watching sadly from the door, and his wife chipping in with 'Good job too! Tha's the last we'll 'ave o' that lot,' I ruthlessly removed dozens of yellowing pictures, ranging in age and propriety, from Victorian ladies in bloomers to Hollywood starlets in considerably less. Each was held in place by four brass drawing-pins; and every pin pulled out a little cone of plaster, leaving a miniature crater behind.

I filled, scraped and sand-papered till I was ready to scream; but I gritted my teeth and worked on. Goodness knows how many hours it took me. At last it was finished, and with the smug satisfaction of a man who has not skimped the preliminaries

I began to apply the cream and green paint that Charlie's wife had chosen. The job had become an obsession. I was determined to attain perfection. After another three nights' labour it was complete. In the light of the paraffin lamp the three of us stood back and drank it in.

'No more o' they ol' pictures, Charlie,' said his wife.

'No fear!' said Charlie. 'Tha's a real tidy job you've made of un. Call in when you've made up yer bill. Us'll 'ave a bit of a settle up.'

Charlie was not too well off, and I erred on the lenient side. In any case I had taken a special pride in that job. I knocked a few nights later and handed Charlie the bill. He didn't ask me in, which rather surprised me; and when he had gone to fetch the money I put my head round the door. From the wall directly over the range Brigitte Bardot smiled triumphantly back at me from between four brass drawing-pins.

(Summer 1969)

PRIMITIVES IN THE PULPIT

Harry Etherington

Methodism was very strong in Holderness – the flat peninsula between the Yorkshire Wolds and the sea – when I was young in the first decade of the century; and particularly so were the Primitives. Indeed, much later, in 1932 when the Methodists united to become one church, three villages close to where I lived at Keyingham refused to join in, and declared themselves to be Continuing Primitive Methodists. Not only that, but they ensured, with all the neces-

sary formalities that, should they at any future date cease to exist, their property would not fall into the hands of 'those other people'. This they did with enthusiasm, and were the only ones in England so to do.

If you were an emotional type, you tended to be drawn to the Primitives. Rather more staid were the Wesleyans, or so it seemed to us youngsters. The Primitives' camp meetings, held in a paddock with waggons as pulpits on Sunday afternoons, were viewed by us as orgies of impassioned religious fervour, much enjoyed by the faithful, and probably a good practising ground for those who aspired to be local preachers.

Even the Wesleyans liked to be moved by a little restrained fervour. The village schoolmaster, who was a student of religious philosophy, was not really appreciated. 'He never gets worked up,' said one critic.

All the Primitive chapel-goers appeared to us boys to be sincere in their religious attitudes, though the sarcastic comments we heard in the village at times, comparing the activities of some of them during the week with the 'umbrella-and-white-collar' behaviour on Sundays, led us to have doubts.

There was a minister in charge of each district, but most services were taken by local worthies whose names appeared on the printed roster (known as 'The Plan') because of their proved ability to preach. And rough-hewn individualistic characters they were, these men I listened to so often on Sunday evenings. Many had little formal education, some spoke only the Holderness dialect, and nearly all were highly emotional in their delivery. They strove valiantly to convert us from our errant ways.

Appearances went to show that they were successful, or so it seemed to us irreligious boys, for their discourses were punctuated by calls of 'Amen!' or 'Praise the Lord!', and by the frequency and loudness of these interjections we measured the response. A preacher received in silence could be sure that he had failed.

We youngsters were always hopefully interested in what the preacher was wearing, for there were several items that could play him false before the end, if he waxed too gesticulatory. His shirt appeared to be a stiffly starched white one, but what we saw was only a false front, hiding the more homely garment of striped print beneath. Or it could be a combination of false front and collar, shaped like a pair of sheep-shears, closed by a stud in the middle or a spring clip at the bottom. Both types were supposed to be held in place by the waistcoat, but this did not always happen, with results that were amusing to us, though to all appearance ignored by the adults. To go with the white front was a tall white collar, usually a choker fitted close up to the chin. Of one particularly short and skinny individual who appeared only head-and-shoulders above the rostrum, my irreverent friend whispered, "Ee leaks like a ferrit peepin' oot of a rabbit ooal'.

Then there were cuffs. Everybody wore cuffs on Sundays, even if (for the boys) they were only celluloid. For the men they were of course starched, though again they were not part of the shirt, but just pushed over the wrist into the sleeve of the jacket, which in normal circumstances was enough to hold them in place. These garments were essential wear for the men when they got togged-up of an evening to go to a Friday night whist drive and dance, or chapel on Sundays. Shirts did not have collars or cuffs, only neckbands and wristbands which were always buttoned up. They were only changed once a week, normally on Saturday night, but Friday if there was a dance. By the end of the week (for they were slept in as well as worked in) they were well ready for the wash, especially if one was a farm worker, as most villagers were.

Attaching a stiffly-starched collar to the shirt by means of a stud passing through the neckband at the back, then bending it round to another stud which was already holding the starched bib at the front, was usually a prolonged acrobatic performance,

'His cuffs . . . flew out over the congregation below him . . .' (Kenneth Mahood)

often ending in profanity and calls for assistance.

There was one long-remembered incident told round the village with delight and exaggerated gesture, of the preacher telling in vigorous language the story of Shadrach, Meshach, and Abed-nego. Towards the peroration his voice rose to a higher pitch as he declared: 'An' these three brave men, Shadrach, Meshach and Abendigo [*sic*] were thrust into the fiery furnace,' and, lapsing further into dialect, 'an' the fire – an' the fire – got yather an' yather – yather an' yather,' and at each phrase he threw out his arms with fists clenched. Then almost screaming his final utterance he proclaimed: 'An' not a hair of ther' 'eads was swinged!' With that he made a last triumphant gesture, but he made it this time with hands outstretched, and his cuffs, which until then had been restrained by his fists, flew out over the congregation below him.

This was a calamity we knew about, but what happened at prayer-meetings, held after the evening services, we never knew, for we were not old enough nor delinquent enough to be allowed to stay. The appeal was made at the end of the service to those who felt their sins bearing heavily upon them, to stay and be 'saved'. What being 'saved' meant we never knew, but we noticed that the ones who stayed were the reprobates and the Saturday-night drunkards, who were known to all. We came to doubt the efficacy of these meetings as the same reprobates were gossiped about week after week, and the same drunks continued their Saturday-night indulgence.

The Primitives were great believers in the power of prayer. After a hymn there would be the first and longest prayer, not read from a book but spoken from the heart. It often went on until every possibility of local mishap and every world-wide calamity had been covered. After another hymn, there would be a second prayer to deal with individual errors and the wayward thoughts to which we were apparently only too prone.

One rugged individual, a pig jobber, gave an instance of what prayer had done for him. He told how he had lost his wife two years before, resulting in his abject misery, which he described eloquently. 'So,' he said, 'in finish I got doon on mi knees, an' I said: "Noo Lord: You mun find me another wife. First 'un was nobbit a semmit 'un".'

The 'find' is here pronounced to rhyme with 'sinned'. 'First' sounded more like 'fust' and 'semmit' is a dialect word meaning 'weak' or 'frail', 'easily broken'. Notice too the fine discrimination in the use of the word 'You'. One never 'thou'd' anybody except God and one's inferiors. Here in his prayer the pig jobber was speaking not to God as the Almighty, but to his Lord and intimate friend.

My dear remembrance, over-riding all else, of those Sunday evenings is of congregations roused, as often happened, to religious ecstasy by the passion of the preacher. There was Westmorland the shoemaker, old Seymour the drainage expert, and many more like them, as conscientious in their worship as in their daily avocations, apparently so devout that in another age they could have been happy in a monastic life. They were assiduous in the avoidance of sin, and 'chapel' gave them the emotional stimulus they needed.

It has been said that great movements are sustained not by thought but by feeling, and when nearly thirty years later I listened to Hitler ranting, and saw his followers at Nuremberg chanting *'Sieg Heil'*, I thought again of those village worshippers who, leading such humdrum lives during the week, were so bewitched sometimes on Sunday that they could have gone to the stake for their beliefs. You should have heard them singing their favourite hymns. I remember them repeating, not twice, but five or six times over before they could leave it, so intoxicated were they, that soul-stirring refrain: 'My chains fell off, My heart was free. I rose, O Lord, and followed Thee.'

(Spring 1984)

THE HELLYMENTAL

Judith Masefield *recorded this story in the words of the Berkshire labourer from whose lips she heard it.*

It was shortly after marriage the queer thing happened. It was our first baby, you see, Miss, and I was in a terrible takin' like young fathers always is. I set off paddin' down lane to fetch the doctor just as soon as me work was done. I bangs his door-knocker and pulls his bell like a Christmas ringer in the belfry. No answer. I nips round to back door and hollers. Coachman pokes his head out. 'Wife's keeled out,' I pants.

'Doctor's been to a house what's had a

visit from the spotted fever,' coachman says. 'It's a midwife you be in need of,' and he roars with laughter.

It was duskish and he lent me an old carriage lantern and I gallops off with anxiety weighin' me down like a mountain. I runs down lane with the mud boundary wall topped with thatch. Summat come out of the wall and flop to the ground with a bump and I thought me heart would tear itself out like an eagle burstin' its cage. It were taller than a donkey and blackish and slimy and rather like a big slug if you get me meanin', a slug with a pig snout, snufflin' all wet and weepy like it had a cold. I hears a soft thud like a sack droppin'. I was dead sure it weren't up to no good and I shines me lantern up to its face and sees its likkle sneaky black eyes and it see me. Dang me, if it didn't start to walk along of me. Not walk exactly, no you couldn't call it walk for it hadn't no feet but a kind of plop-puddle-swish on its bottom end, the awfulest sort of thing you could hope to see, and I couldn't shake it off nohow. 'I won't do you no 'arm,' I says, and it bends its squashy waist and goes sniffle-snuffle down its porker snout and me legs turns soft and lantern blows out.

When I reaches midwife's cottage I faints dead out on the door stone. The good woman props me up and says as she fears I'm in me death shiver. 'Whatever be you at?' she says ever so kindly. 'A baby ain't the thing to get that way over.'

'It ain't baby,' I says holdin' me heart together with both hands, 'it be that pappy bolster of a slug what come follerin' me through the village with a cold in its nose, goin' sniffle-snuffle.'

'Fancy a big man like you bein' frit by such a thing,' midwife says and starts to laugh. 'Why, it's popped out of wall at me many a time.'

'Whatever would you go for to call it?' I says as me breath begun to blow in me lungs again.

'It's what they calls a hellymental,' she says. 'You don't need to get pannicky over they. Say the Lord's Prayer. No wickedness won't stand up before that.'

'But it comes from the pit,' I says. 'I never knowd before as there was such cattle. What were it? If you knows, tell me.'

'You knows of Jim Jackson, what lived by slaughter house?' she says. 'It weren't nothin' more nor less than his wickedness. He was one of they what don't believe in God. A haytheist they calls 'em. It were all he'd done wrong gathered itself together into a bag. That's all it were.'

She come along of me and brought her goodness and baby come easy as easy. I'd 'ad me warnin' though. I minded me life after that.

(Winter 1966)

ROADSIDE ENCOUNTER

Muiris MacEanruig

I met the old couple only once, in Perthshire. Their low humped tent was pitched under the trees at the roadside, rather uncomfortably close, I thought, to the traffic roaring by. Why did they not choose a quieter spot, over a hillock or in the quarry? In the lulls it was pleasant enough here by their tinkers' fire with birds singing, foliage rustling and somewhere a burn chuckling; but then would come another car.

'We went tae London once,' said the old man, smiling as he whittled a stick. 'Walked a' the wey.'

'Walked!'

'Ay, we hiv a son doon there. He has a guid job. He married a girl frae London when he was in the airmy. He was aye askin' us doon and askin' us doon. So one day we up and goes. Ye see that wee pram? We pushed it a' the wey doon and back.'

I looked at the pram, small, low and old-fashioned, the kind for which many tinkers find a use long after the bairns are up. 'How long,' I asked, 'did it take you to go down?'

They could not remember. They did not stay long in London: the son's wife, it seemed, did not make them over-welcome. So they soon started back again. It was late spring, and in the north of England snow fell. They put up their tent and waited for it to stop. On the second evening an old shepherd came down and spoke to them in their little hole in a snowdrift; and the following day he brought them a large home-cured ham.

'Did you enjoy it?' I inquired.

They laughed: 'Och, we never ate it. We pit it on the fire. We had nae sticks y'see.' The old woman's eyes glowed with the memory of it. 'It made a braw fire. Burned for two nichts and two days. It was a rare warm tent that.'

She had been brewing tea in a can suspended over the flames. Now she handed me a steaming cup, which I sipped gratefully. As I drank it, they told me that for some years they had confined their travels to this fifteen-mile stretch of road. Their elder son had been in the Air Force during the war, and his plane had been shot down. He had been reported missing, believed killed. 'But he's no deid,' said the old man firmly, 'and this is the road he'll come lookin' for us by. We were aye here when him and his brither was laddies. They was brocht up alang this road.'

(Winter 1959)

FOXGLOVES FOR THE WAR EFFORT

D. M. Thomas

In 1940, my husband being unfit for active service, we became foxglove-farmers. The medicine digitalis is derived from this flower (its Latin name is *Digitalis purpurea*) and was urgently needed to treat cases of heart disease and shell-shock.

We rented a cottage at Ruan High Lanes near Truro. In an adjoining shed, my husband fitted racks of netting on which the foxglove leaves were dried by two braziers. To gather them we bicycled around the lanes, finding that foxgloves grew with special abundance where farmers had recently rebuilt the Cornish stone 'hedges'.

Our biggest problem was obtaining coke for the braziers. The leaves had to be tinder-dry or they would be rejected by the herbalist (Ransome of Hitchin, Hertford-

Foxgloves. (E. Deuchars)

THE BRAMBLES REMEMBER

She has gone, but I think
That the brambles still remember
The feel of her hand
Touching their thorny arms tenderly;
Touching their autumn-leafed
Crimsoned golden splendour,
Leaving their berries intact
For the children to see.
I think she knew that the
Growing things love touching
By fingers that would never bruise or
    tear.
She has gone, but I think these
    hedgerows
Will remember
How gentle she was, how she loved
    them when she was there.
       Aileen E. Passmore (Autumn 1977)

shire) who paid us 1s. 9d. per lb. This gave us an income of about £5 a week. After a couple of years a firm of medical suppliers asked us to manage a farm at Ladcock, a few miles away, growing cultivated fox-gloves, which yield a stronger drug.

(Spring 1986)

JUBILEE JANE

D. Macer Wright

Jubilee Jane lived in a small thatched round-house at the end of a lane bordered by high banks and elms. In spring the banks were starred with celandine and wood anemone; throughout the summer they knew drifts of cow parsnip, and late into October the toadflax bloomed. Over the hedge poppies rioted among the corn, and we often found the beautiful and now vanished corn cockle, for this was before science decreed that wild flowers shall no longer grace field and hedgerow.

A visit to Jubilee's cottage was one of the delights of childhood. The parlour with

'Jubilee's small thatched round-house at the end of the lane.' (Brian Walker)

its ceiling blackened by decades of lamp smoke, the old sofa sprouting horsehair and coiled springs, the multitude of china figures, her clay pipes and paper spills, the ancient gramophone with its vast horn and the thrill of being in a room that was completely round: all lent the place the magic of an Aladdin's cave.

Her musical taste was simple: negro spirituals, something about an old cow-hand, and a piece that ran:

Oh, a million miles I've travelled
And a million sights I've seen,
And I'm longing for the glory soon to be.

They comprised her collection, together with a record of chamber music which, she said, she played only to the quality. The

'She snatched up the pudding and thrust it between the bars of the grate . . .' (Brian Walker)

noise that came through the horn when this was played cannot be described. Music means different things to different people; to Jubilee Jane it meant the comfort of a nice little weep.

She had a passion for cold bread-pudding and elderberry wine. The pudding was kept, for reasons not immediately apparent, underneath the sofa. There it held company with her two slumbering cats who, with the fastidiousness of their kind, showed no liking for such plebeian fare. That bread-pudding remains as one of the vivid memories of days long gone. Jubilee cut a piece and placed it before me, then went outside to get some wine. 'Quick,' hissed my mother, 'into the fire'; and she snatched up the pudding and thrust it between the bars of the grate. It sizzled and spat and gave out curious odours; the currants glared balefully before they became cinders. By the grace of Providence Jubilee was a long time fetching the wine. When she returned the pudding was in its death throes, and my mother was standing before the fire, smiling and pulling at her stays.

Life with its country winds and its privations had left many marks on Jubilee's face. Yet laughter, too, had cut deep. For, though an ageing washerwoman with a taste for the bottle and a rough tongue that could still speak its own kind of poetry, she had that greatest of blessings, good humour. She was something of a rarity among Christians for, if she could not say good of her neighbour, she said nothing.

In full fig and ready to do battle with the flagstone floor of the public bar, Jubilee was no ordinary spectacle. The most striking feature was her scarlet bloomers. Into these she would tuck her skirts before commencing to punish the floor with bucket and mop. On a hot morning of high summer she would plunge her feet into the bucket, 'jest to cool me bunions'.

Saturday nights would find her punishing the same floor but in a different manner. Then her bloomers brought to the gloomy precincts of the bar a much needed touch of colour. Into them her skirts were again tucked, and she would perform wild gypsy jigs to the accompaniment of foot-stamping, whistling, banging of tankards and vocal pandemonium. In vain would the landlord plead, though truth to tell he would have been a disappointed man if Jubilee had ceased to grace his bar, for she brought good trade. 'Orlright now, Jube gel. That'll do, blast it.' But the jigging Jubilee, flushed with a good measure of stout laced with gin, was in no mood to be dictated to by a mere landlord, and on went the dance.

She would have found little point of contact with today's helps who, we are told, only do it to oblige. There was no obliging about Jubilee. She scrubbed other people's floors and washed their dirty linen

'Wild gypsy jigs . . .' (Brian Walker)

because she had to live, and because she found it easier than the back-breaking field work she had done in her youth. Then she must have belonged to the line of that sun-blackened company who walked the lanes of Jefferies' Wiltshire in their 'rags and jags', but who had a beauty that seemed to have sprung from their native landscape. For Jubilee, grotesque perhaps in her scarlet knickers, still had a merry eye and a warm lip. And when she had scrubbed a floor or washed a sheet, these things were more than just clean. They took on a brilliance that made a dull day bright. Many an eye lingered over Jubilee's sheets blowing in the wind; many a boot paused at the edge of her stone floors.

Jubilee Jane had a sharp nose, but it never poked itself into other people's business; she had capacious hands, but nothing that did not belong to her ever found its way into them. She neither expected nor received more than the worth of her hire, and throughout her life she gave more than she received. As a good Samaritan she held a place which people far better endowed would find hard to occupy. She would trudge the lanes and fields to leave a basketful of what she called 'greens' outside the door of someone old and ailing, and she spent more than one night with a neighbour whose husband was screaming the house down in delirium tremens. She knew of herbs and strange potions; she was weather-wise and had green fingers. Her knowledge would have confounded a B.B.C. brains trust. It was learned not from books but from the meadows and woods in rain and sun, in the iron of winter as well as in the picnic time of summer; not that Jubilee had much time for picnics.

She ended her days in what was euphemistically known as a 'home'. The possibility of such an ending was one of the few things that haunted her later days. 'I'd sooner die in a shed in me own back garden,' she told my mother. But she was taken away from the round-house one day when chiffchaffs were busy in the lane. Her pipes and spills they left behind. My mother took in her two cats, but they went wild after a few days.

In her fashion Jubilee Jane had given life and laughter to the village. She had brought it the brightness of her bloomers, and she had kept bright its linens and its stone floors. When she had gone there was a sort of mournful peace in the public bar. Her place in the churchyard was marked by no stone, only a mound of earth. Had there been a stone, it might have borne the legend: 'Jubilee Jane, about whom the wagging tongues could find no ill to speak'.

I went back recently to that once remote village. The elms are down in Jubilee's lane. Where the round-house stood there is a broiler battery. The pub where she danced is bedizened with strip lighting. But in the straggly corner of a field, once the bottom of her garden, is a bent and lichened tree still bearing scarlet fruits. It is the Siberian crab we planted together. She insisted on setting it with its main roots pointing to windward, assuring me that it would then never blow down.

(Summer 1966)

TAIL CORN

Devon shop assistant, looking out at the rain: 'Fair gives 'ee moolligroobs, doan't un?' *(Summer 1952)*

Dorset dairyman's son, asked, after a lesson on the Channel Isles, to name the islands: 'Jersey, Guernsey, Alderney, and' – after much deliberation – 'Shartarn'. *(Summer 1950)*

Northumbrian, of a woman whose achievement does not always match her promises: 'She dissent aalways flee when she flops 'er wings.' *(Spring 1957)*

Footpath to Old Amersham, Bucks. (Laurence E. Perkins)

FRED'S LITTLE RED BUS

Don Hogg

The wonder of the age sixty years ago for the village people of Ruscombe, near Stroud, in Gloucestershire, was to get a bus from the town. Until this arrived in the 1920s, they had to walk five or six miles to their jobs before it was even first light, and walk back again after a hard day's graft.

The bus was privately owned by an Australian who had returned from the 1914–18 war. The driver was Fred Edgeworth, a young fellow who had been driving his brother-in-law's lorries since he was fifteen. It was only a very small bus, with fourteen wooden seats. It was painted red, with a kangaroo on each side, and it soon became known as the Meat Box, with a cheerful young red-haired driver to match it.

The fares on the little red bus ranged from 1d. to 3d. and it was used every day, during the week for workers and shoppers and for Saturday football teams or Sunday School outings. In his wages at the weekend, Fred would collect an extra 2s. 6d. for every 400 passengers carried on his bus during his thirteen to seventeen trips a day. There were no timetables – or tickets. As money was not so plentiful in those days, Fred often had to 'chalk up' the fares of hard-up passengers. Nevertheless, they were all hard-working and proud village people, and they would pay up every weekend.

Fred was liked for miles around, and the ladies of the village loved him so much that on very cold days they would bring him out cups of hot tea – too many on some trips. It meant that Fred had to stop the bus and go dodging behind some old building, far too often for his liking, but the villagers didn't seem to mind a bit.

The journey from Stroud started at Lansdown, through to cheerful places aptly named Puck's Hole Harbour, Humphrey's End, Watery Lane, Sugar Hole, Breadstreet, Primrose Hill, Ludlow Green, Middle Spring, bottom of Zion Hill Pitch, and on to Honest Corner, the bus terminus, where regular customers were picked up. Some of the village housewives were running a mail order club which had just started up; they ordered items from the glossy catalogues. Many of these would come by rail, and Fred was called upon to be the carrier of the goods. Parcels were left at the Painswick Inn, at the end of Gloucester Street, for Fred to collect with a reward of 'something for a drink'. At one time, he had seventy-two drinks to his credit, all paid for by the locals.

He would also call at Lewis & Godfrey's haberdashery shop in the town, for cottons and silks for the three smart dressmaker sisters who lived in Humphrey's End. For his trouble, he would receive a cup of tea and a copper or two for his pocket. Sometimes Fred brought up the beer for the local pub and the wet fish for the fishmonger, down in the Clover, at Honest Corner. From these traders Fred had a glass of beer and a bag of chips.

Fred was a very skilful driver; he had to be to negotiate the very narrow roads, often skimming the hedgerows and nearly scraping the old stone walls of gardens and cottages. A special spot of driving was

THE COUNTRY BUS

How like an old, long-married pair
They were, sitting sedate and small
On a front seat, he with an arm
Round her shoulder, holding her there
As if to enclose her from harm;
And neither talking at all.

And when the bus stopped, how he
    guided her
With a stately, old-fashioned care;
She might have been blind, but her eyes
Were alive with delight at the stir
Of the market-day crowd. I'd surmise
He was ten, the wiser perhaps by a
    year.
                    Diana Mann (Spring 1983)

'The baker would stand on the wall and wave his basket . . .' (Brian Walker)

needed by Holborrow's shop at the Middle Spring; it was a very tight squeeze to get the tiny bus through. One memorable time found the Co-op Bakery roundsman, with his horse and cart, meeting up with the little bus at Watery Lane. After that an arrangement was made between the driver and the drover that the baker would stand on the wall and wave his bread basket at the top of Water Lane to indicate that Fred could come on up the hill. If the baker wasn't there waving his basket, then it was a warning to Fred, that the horse and cart were on their way down.

Fred's last journey on a Saturday night was around eleven o'clock. He would wait in town for the couples to come out from the Picture Palace. The lovers were brought home safe and sound and dropped off at their respective spots to kiss and cuddle and say their goodnights.

During 1927, when Fred was driving the little red bus from Stroud to Ruscombe, a pretty passenger called Phyllis would often accompany him just for a ride. Fred married Phyllis one August morning in 1928. He drove the usual late bus to Ruscombe the night before the wedding, which was to take place at the Old Chapel in Stroud at 9 a.m. This particular night, the villagers were waiting for Freddie to pull up at the Honest Corner terminus. They presented him with a handsome chair, and a half tea-service, bought with coppers given by the locals. In the chair they sat Fred, who mildly protested, and carried him shoulder-high around the village. The bus was filled with flowers for his bride, and Fred was filled with ale; then they saw him off, cheerfully weaving his way down to Stroud in the early hours. Next morning, all the Ruscombe villagers turned out, and filled the chapel in Stroud to throw their confetti.

In 1932, the Australian gave up the little red Ruscombe bus, and the Red & White Company ran it until 1950, when it was taken over by the Western National and eventually by the Bristol Omnibus Company. Fred continued to journey the hills, and in 1960 he was promoted to inspector, and later he was made station inspector at the bus station in Stroud. He retired in 1971 after forty-five years in the transport service.

Fred was one of the best, and greatly liked by the staff of the bus services in Stroud, and into his retirement he took the best wishes of a host of friends.

(Spring 1984)

LIGHT OF OTHER DAYS

Freda Turner

Hermitage Hilfield Leigh, Wootton Glanville, Long Burton with Holnest, Buckland Newton with Plush: these were the Dorset names I used to hear as I sat, a small child, in the thrilling hooded gloom of the carrier's van, jolting and rumbling over the rough road to Sherborne market and listening to the women's talk. That was nearly half a century ago; but the other day, turning out a bookshelf of one who had died, I found these places again as they were when my parents were young. In 1902, with the enterprise proper to the new century and the new reign, this group of villages began jointly to produce a parish magazine: not the customary clutch of notices, forming a mere cover round some impersonal mass-produced church publication, but a quarterly journal devoted wholly to the parishes concerned.

How long *Home News* continued to be published I do not know; but one reader at least kept all the issues for ten years or so, and then had them bound. I think it may have been my grandfather – blacksmith, sexton and grave-digger – who went to this expense; or perhaps it was my grandmother. She had her own resources, thanks to the sweet-shop she kept in the parlour and to the gloves she stitched at home for a Yeovil factory and then put under the chair cushion, where they would certainly be pressed in due course by some neighbour, sitting there and telling her troubles. I do not know whose hand put a bookmarker between the pages, so that they open at a piece headed 'A Pretty Wedding'. The bridegroom is the vicar's gardener, the bride 'the much appreciated Mistress of the Infant School': my father and mother. It is

August 1903. The world as they know it will last exactly eleven more years.

But *Home News* starts earlier, and with home-comings. By twos and threes, soldiers are returning from South Africa to Long Burton, Hilfield, Plush; to be admired in their khaki and welcomed by church bells, thanksgiving services, speeches and handsome silver watches. A baby's name on the Leigh baptismal register is Ladysmith Mary Guppy. The obsequies for the lamented Queen are not long over when everyone is in church again, praying for the King's recovery. Village committees are plunged in controversy because of the postponed coronation: whether to go ahead with the old folk's dinner but let the children wait for their tea, whether to hand out the commemoration medals right away but keep back the prayer-books, whether to hang out a few flags or none. Luckiest is the committee which is able to report that it has managed to postpone everything for the time being 'without the loss of any of the contributions'.

With trains stopping at Yetminster, people going to Canada as casually as though it were Dorchester and the postman calling regularly even at Hermitage, nobody complains about rural isolation; and nobody boasts about it either. These are still the plain and unselfconscious years in the countryside. Sophisticated strangers are not yet trying to buy the lovely old Ham-stone farmhouses, and nobody has yet moved into one of the thatched cottages to write a townsman's book about the country. The villages still belong to themselves.

In each of the parishes the vicar gets copy ready for *Home News*, four times a year. The parish register entries from the village are included: baptisms, marriages, burials. Three-score and ten are as many

years as most people hope for at this time, when the seventies, or even the sixties, represent a reasonably ripe old age. Many die younger and, reading the names half a century later, one guesses that the young man or woman succumbed to tuberculosis, the result of growing up in a large, poor, underfed, underdoctored family in a farm labourer's damp and over-crowded cottage; that the married woman in her thirties died from unskilled midwifery, leaving, besides one dead baby, a house full of living children.

Infant mortality is more than five times, maternal mortality more than seven times, what they will be fifty years later; and with so many lives making a shaky start the tendency is to take precautions. To judge from *Home News* the practice of private baptism is commoner than it will be later on. One can imagine the panic and piety in the poor mother's bedroom as the vicar, by the wash-basin, hastily gives a name to a brief life which appears already to be nearly over. But though the name of a privately baptised baby sometimes occurs again straight away among the burials, it is not always so: there are miscalculations. I know that, before I come to the end, I am going to find myself privately baptised at one day old. Our family is indeed a great help to one parish register during these years; for my mother, no longer teaching other people's infants, produces five of her own and loses two of them before she is thirty.

Another regular source of copy is the school. Perfect attendance is of first importance, and those who achieve it get medals, albums of photographs and a sight of their names in print. The reports of the diocesan inspector on the state of religious teaching in the national schools are uniformly good:

[75]

(Brian Walker)

The teaching power in the school is excellent . . . the infants answered brightly and with intelligence, and many thoughtful answers were given by the upper standards . . . the discipline and tone are very good . . . the singing is distinct, and the repetition was said intelligently.

The Board of Education inspectors, reporting on what the vicar calls 'secular work', are slightly less enthusiastic. Moreover they are given to pointing out the need for improvements in the premises: walls to be decorated, floors to be relaid. One school requires 'sanitary arrangements' (probably earth-closets) which will cost £14; and, as the vicar rather glumly points out, 'this money will not come out of the rates'. But then he drops the subject, and rightly, for in spite of the careful compromises of Balfour's 1902 Act the 'Church question' is still dynamite in the field of education. If the Church pays for earth-closets and other things at the National School, it is (as the vicar well knows) to maintain the right to

teach the pupils the catechism. And if the Nonconformist children go to the National School it is not that they have any use for the catechism but that, as in many another rural area, this is the only school. Peace in such a complex situation is surely cheap at £14.

Yet, though there is mention of one child's being withdrawn from Scripture lessons under the conscience clause, Nonconformists and Church people are generally on the best of terms in these villages. In Leigh they go to the same Bible class, where (says the vicar) 'we are already learning to know each other better'. The vicar leads the parish in mourning the death of a Wesleyan neighbour 'to whom we largely owe the absence of all bitterness'. In Buckland the Nonconformists join with the Church people in a farewell presentation to a well-loved vicar on account of his 'unfailing courtesy, kindliness and good feeling towards all'.

'A farewell presentation to a well-loved vicar . . .'
(Brian Walker)

When he comes to reporting his general parish news each vicar finds the chance to turn journalist. The contributions vary in style, as no doubt the sermons do; yet they have a flavour in common not only with each other but with the literary products of other country parsonages at other times.

> Alas! again a goodbye is before us. May Osmond, a sweet sunny-tempered girl of some thirteen summers, is leaving Minterne with her parents for Cattistock. The child is beloved by all, not least by ourselves, and the Sunday School will feel greatly when the brown-eyed, rosy-cheeked maiden comes no more. We hope May will keep a corner for us in her warm little heart.

It is uncanny to find this, not in the diaries of the Rev. Francis Kilvert, who has been dead since 1879 and whose notebooks are not going to see the light of day till 1938, but in the pages of a Dorset parish magazine in 1909.

There is no writing down to the readers of *Home News*. Probably nobody minds an occasional little scholarly flourish, coming from an educated man. The village of Long Burton may well wonder at the first message sent along the telegraph wire which links it to Sherborne:

> Nuntius aligeris hodie fulgoribus actus
> Incipit hinc nostrum transvolitare polum.

But at least *Home News* provides this translation: 'A message hence, by winged lightnings driven, Today begins to fly across our heaven.' Farmer Fox and Farmer Green may find themselves described as 'our kindly Jehus' when they lend their time and wagons to take the children on the Sunday School treat, and little Fanny Matthews may read to her surprise, how she was 'almost captured by Neptune' while sitting on Weymouth beach.

The Sunday School, the Mothers' Meeting, the choir – all go to 'the English Naples' (Weymouth) year after year for the annual outing. The horse-drawn wagons, decorated with green branches, take the singing cheering crowds to the station and fetch them home.

> And who shall tell the delights of paddling, the Nothe, the heavy gun practice, the out-going and in-coming Channel Island steamers, the excellent tea?

The donkeys are always up to expectation. A bazaar with everything at 6¾d. so delights the mothers that they nearly miss their train. Nobody bathes; and though there is a good deal of paddling, there cannot be as much as one report would have us believe:

> Our girls take to the water like fish, and leaving shoes and stockings in charge of sympathetic teachers, they spent the warm sunny hours wading knee deep, nay waist deep . . .

But this, of course, is nonsense.

Dorset is nearly all grass-growing country at this time. Every fork-full of hay is precious, and until the crop is off the cricket field, towards the end of July, the

(Brian Walker)

team must find somewhere else to play. It plays just the same. Someone lends a poor pasture with no hay on it, someone gets busy with horse and roller, and by fair means or foul the captain finds eleven men. 'Probably we lost,' writes one club secretary after a disappointing season, 'because they were better teams; but our rule of playing resident members only makes it very hard on so small a parish, especially when it is not recognised by our opponents.' Among the legitimate indigenous players who honourably lose so many matches I see young men whom I shall know later as uncles and cousins, and later still as names on war memorials. These young men also ring the church bells, do 'readings', sing to the banjo at concerts and go round ringing hand-bells on Christmas Eve.

Various clubs flourish in the villages. Chess matches last into the early hours. The curiously named Labourers' Encouragement Society gives 10s. to the father sending the greatest number of children regularly to Sunday School. People save through the coal and clothing clubs and get a bonus which is provided by local benefactors. One of them withdraws his charitable contribution promptly when the education rate goes up.

Old age pensions – 5s. a week for needy people over seventy – are inaugurated on 1 January, 1909 and hailed 'with much pleasure by the recipients, whatever may be the feelings of those from whose pockets the requisite millions of pounds sterling will be extracted to pay the bill'. But some of the old people are still able to heap coals of fire; and more than one vicar has soon to report the receipt of various small sums – sixpences, shillings, halfcrowns – to be placed in the missionary box as thank-offerings from old age pensioners.

What with runaway horses, angry bulls and a growing number of reckless cyclists, male and female, there is nearly always a crop of accidents to report. A woman faints while drawing water from a well, falls in, but is pulled out alive. A little girl, putting a kettle on the fire, is burned to death. An astonishing number of people manage to fall out of, or under, wagons.

At this time one sees in print things which will later be ruled out absolutely. 'We hear he has left a moderate fortune,' says one vicar concerning a departed parishioner; and another parson, reporting a village funeral which almost coincides with that of Edward VII, remarks that 'the labourers' task truly was over, and our mighty Edward and lowly Carpenter both laid down their earthly burden for the crown of rest'.

There is not much sermonising in *Home News*, but now and then the Bishop of Salisbury administers a pastoral rebuke: 'We tolerate sins of impurity more readily and have an even lower standard than the last generation in books, plays and newspapers, perhaps even in conversation.' Impartially he reproves all social classes. The poor, he says, are particularly addicted to gambling and intemperance, and 'too many servants fail to make their masters' interest their own and rob them of time and service, if not of goods and money'. As for the rich, 'too many employers are careless of the religious and moral life of their servants'. What Bishop Wordsworth thinks of the low wages, the high rates of infant and maternal mortality and the thousands of tumble-down cottages in his diocese he does not say.

The rush to Canada gathers speed during these years. As many as four sons may go from one family. Fathers and mothers get letters, which are printed in 'Home News', about life in lumber camps, big pay, empty acres for sale, bears and wild cats and snow. In Dorset the pace of life quickens. While denying that he is about to make drastic innovations, a new vicar is bold enough to say that he thinks a surpliced choir 'might be desirable in a few years' time'. The last of the old village nurses dies. A District Nursing Association comes into being; a trained and certificated nurse arrives. Somebody counts as many as forty bicycles outside the hedge at Leigh fête. Cars, as yet always called motor-cars, grow commoner. In 1908 Buckland has a motor-car wedding, timed for two o'clock, but the bridegroom waits in the church, the bride at home; there is a dreadful delay while the motor-car will not move, and it is 2.52 p.m. when the bride arrives, 'just in time to be wedded within the legal hours'.

Nearly at the end of this volume of *Home News* the soldiers come suddenly, as if from nowhere – 15,000 of them. There is mimic war round Sherborne and the villagers have the time of their lives. But for me, a ghost returned from the unimaginable future, the white tents are spread eerily over Wootton Common like a shroud; and I feel I have no more right among these happy unsuspecting people – knowing what I know.

(Autumn 1961)

PARTY LINE

Gladys E. Robson

When we bought our cottage it had no gas, electricity or main drainage. The great bait was the telephone, which is more than a luxury when you have just left London and are living seven miles from a town; but the day after we moved in the line was dead and post office engineers could not trace the fault. Then one day I got through and sighed with relief. My satisfaction was short-lived, for next day the line was dead again. So I decided to go and see the subscriber with whom I shared it.

I felt that I was under observation as I walked up the pathway, but there was no reply to my knock. Then I looked at the little dark window near the door and saw an eye peeping round the curtain – an unblinking shoe-button eye. I addressed myself to it, asking if I might speak to the owner. The eye continued to inspect me, then disappeared. Presently an upstairs window opened to reveal the funniest little figure of a woman, very short and fat, with an old grey scarf round her neck and chin and a square tea-cosy hat of shaggy fur.

'Good morning,' I said. 'Can you please tell me if you have a telephone here?'

There was no answer, and the button eyes continued to stare. I tried again, explaining that I was the new lady from the thatched cottage up the hill and believed that I shared her telephone line. At last she spoke: 'I don't know nothing about it.'

Once more I told my story and, as I did so, I began to feel I was babbling. Then she spoke again: 'I don't hold with it.' That was all I got out of her before I cycled home, rather shaken.

There was deadlock for three months, during which the line was sometimes alive for a week and, for no apparent reason, went dead again. Then I suddenly realised that, when I tried to telephone, the noise on the line was similar to that made when a receiver is left off. I told the engineers, who visited the old lady and asked to see her telephone. They found it on the floor in a corner behind a chair – with the receiver off. She told them that she was only caretaking for owners abroad and was afraid of telephones. If the bell rang she unhooked the receiver and left it dangling, perhaps for a week or more. Then, when she thought it was behaving, she would put it back till the next call came through. In the end I was given a separate line.

(Winter 1957)

EARLY TELEPHONE DAYS

Beatrice Reid

Sixty years ago we lived near Brighton and there was no telephone in the village, so my father wrote to the manager of the Bell Telephone Company to say there were several people who wanted one. The reply was that a line from the Brighton exchange would be connected if he would guarantee twelve subscribers. The annual charge would be £3 for unlimited local calls. Installation would be free, and there was no such thing as rental. We soon got our twelve subscribers including the doctor, the grocer, the butcher and the major, a retired cavalry officer whose chief occupation was backing horses.

There was much speculation as to where the exchange would be, and this was settled a few weeks later when the butcher's boy announced that the pole for the line from Brighton had arrived. He had seen it that morning on a long trailer drawn by a horse. At that moment men were digging a hole in the backyard of one of the houses in Albert Road. Sure enough the little front room of a terraced house occupied by Mr and Mrs Martin and their baby became the exchange. Mrs Martin was to be our operator. It was not long before the pole was used as a heaven-sent attachment for her neighbours clothes-line, while her own baby's small garments fluttered from the guy cables.

A few more poles appeared in the village as the subscribers were connected, and when our turn came we decided to have the instrument, no ornament on any consideration, in the cloakroom. My father, being a very tall man, had it fixed to the wall to suit his height. This caused a certain amount of annoyance as he was hardly ever at home. A large block of wood was placed on the floor on which the other members of the family stood in order to reach the mouthpiece and turn the handle to call the operator. It had not occurred to anyone at that date to sit down while telephoning. A personal directory hung on a hook near by, until it fell to the floor and was chewed up by one of the dogs. After that numbers were written on the wall around the telephone. The wall could never be repainted.

The large cloakroom was lit by a gas jet. After dark we never knew which should come first, lighting the gas or answering the telephone. Often there were important messages for my father which he insisted should be written down accurately. The room contained the usual paraphernalia; a long wooden box for the croquet set, greatcoats, raincoats, satchels and so forth on the pegs, and a thick fur-lined, camel-haired coat used by my father when driving the dog-cart in winter. It was past its prime, but was reprieved from the jumble sale by my mother who in the cold weather always wore it when telephoning. She told everybody to do this; it was known as the telephone coat.

We all got on well with Mrs Martin. Our first call of the day was frequently preceded by 'How's the baby?' When his first tooth appeared we were duly informed. She knew who our friends were, and would sometimes tell us their whereabouts. Once when I was arranging a tennis four she told me that Miss Wilson had gone to Brighton on the ten and would be back on the twelve. The clatter of crockery was sometimes heard, as though she were making her pastry alongside the switchboard. On one occasion when my sister and I had gone to a party in Brighton, we telephoned home at about midnight to say that we had missed the last train (though actually we had never intended catching it). When we got home next morning my mother told us to pick a basket of strawberries and take it to Mrs Martin with an apology for ringing so late.

Albert, her husband, took over the switchboard on Sundays and some evenings. Albert had a bored, irritated voice, as though we had interrupted him from reading the evening paper. Occasionally we would hear an unfamiliar voice explaining that Mrs Martin had the day off, and that it was her sister speaking. It was all very much a family affair. As time went on we could gauge the age of the baby by the snatches of conversation overheard. At first it was 'Shh, go to sleep like a good boy'. A few months later it would be 'Albert, do come and help. He's kicked the ink over'. At some later date, when inquiring about a trunk call, it was 'George, if you climb on to that table again you'll get a good smacked bottom'.

Then my sister and I went to France for a year to a so-called finishing school. In our absence the General Post Office bought out the Bell Telephone Company, and Mrs Martin's little front room was no longer our exchange. A combined post office and telephone exchange had been built around the corner on the main road. We became a number and nothing more.

(Winter 1972)

IN RURAL DORSET

Evelyn Downs

The last bus back from Bridport would take me no nearer than seven miles to the isolated house where I was staying, and I had been advised to book a taxi for the rest of the journey. On arriving in the town I found a kiosk and searched the directory for the number of a recommended garage at Drimpton, but in vain; neither the present owner's name nor that of his predecessor was listed, and there was no clue in the Drimpton entries. I rang Inquiries, but with no better success. Then

I tried the Broadwindsor post office.

'Sorry,' said a kindly voice, 'I don't know the number myself, though I know the place you want. You could try the people over the road from the garage – or the builder. He'd probably know. Or there's Mrs A. at the farm.'

With a handful of pennies I once more searched the directory. The people over the road were not listed; the builder was out; so I tried the farm. A woman's voice answered.

'My dear, of course you can't walk all that way. Seems strange though; but you're quite right, the name's not there. Well, 'tis a problem. Tell you what, I'll have a scout round and see if I can find it. You give me that number you're ringing from and I'll call you back.'

I went outside to wait, realising that an hour of my precious day had gone already. In due course the kiosk telephone rang.

'Hello – is that the lady that wants the Drimpton garage? Sorry to have been so long. I couldn't find the number, so I popped out into the road in case anybody passing could help. Well, my dear, you'll laugh when I tell you. There was a little girl playing outside, so I asked her to run home and see if her mother knew the number of the garage. "I don't need to," she said; "I know that number. 'Tis on the parish magazines." So here 'tis, if you'll just write it down. Goodbye, my dear; glad I was able to help.'

(Winter 1962)

THE POST

Wendy Wood

Rab, the regular postman of Glenbog, was taking his late autumn holiday, so the job had to be done by someone else in the glen. Tommy Beag leaned across the counter of the tiny post office and thereby revealed the reason for his nickname Small. 'Well, Andrew, I could do the post round, yes,' he agreed. 'But I could wish it were summer, for myself and the pony will not be any earlier from the railway station than Rab was, and that will be five o'clock and it dark. I hope there'll not be too many parcels. I don't like them parcels. Long ones like corsets for Bella, and ones marked "Glass" all over for the Big House.'

It was indeed no small undertaking: the railhead was eight miles away along a bridle-track, and on return the pony was left in the post-office field and the letters delivered on foot. For a week Tommy enjoyed the cups of tea at the many crofts, and the importance of being the bearer from the outside world of news which lost nothing of drama in its inaccuracy. On the Thursday he had left a good supper simmering in the iron pot beside the peat fire in his cottage, a combined poaching effort having resulted in a generous distribution of venison; but that night he did not return to eat it. He lived alone, so he was not missed till the morning, when somebody heard his cow calling out to be milked and organised a search party.

'It was all the fault of that damned calf of Schokie's,' Tommy complained later. 'I left the bag under a bush at the Gorstan because it was heavier than the few letters left in it; and when I got back, hadn't that hell of a stirk streeled it right across the Auchmor? So I was late and thought I'd take the short cut. It saves nearly a mile that way, up and over the hill, but it's not my side of the glen. I was all right up between the two Big Rocks and down the Lag [hollow] and along the Shelf, and to the Big Flat. Dhia! It was the blackest night ever I saw; but I was all right with the bright torch – that's what I thought. More fool me. For just when I was at the top of Sgurr na Moine [the peat bog] the light got terrible weak. I had two new batteries in, so I thought it might be the spring needed something more of padding. I took a bit paper out of my pocket and sat down on a rock and opened up the torch.

'Man, it was quiet – quiet and black. Up there, backwards to the west and under the shoulder of the hill, there wasn't even the difference of blackness that the sea usually gives. Like being inside a small box it was. The sheep was all low down – no birds. It was worse than the look of the end of the world; you'd think it had never begun. I had the two ends of the torch in my hand. I pushed the spring up – nothing but a wee glim like a *cuileag-shniomhain* [glow-worm]. So I knew it was the bulb that was not screwed down tight, and I undid the top. The silly wee footling pip of a thing! Didn't it fall out of my fingers? I said to me, "Tommy, this is when you don't get flustered", and sat where I was, bending down to feel with my fingers; grass, heather, wee stones, I could feel them all, but no bulb. Then I went on my knees, searching all around, and I prayed, indeed I prayed, for the thought of going back beside the precipice or on by the bog bridge put such fear on me that I was shaking like a *critheann* [aspen].

Postman on horseback near Newmill, just north of Penzance, Cornwall. (Kenneth Scowen)

'But what was the use of sitting there? I could feel the cold eating into my bones. A match? Amadan! Do you think I would not have made a torch of the heather if I'd had a match at me? I was near the panic that tears the head off you; but I knew it was thirteen hours before a glim of daylight, so I just had to go on. You know the bog bridge, the raised curved bit, only twice the width of a foot? If there had just been a star or two; but there was a drizzle of cloud and no sky. Daft-like I shouted, and my voice melted just in front of my face. I felt as if I was the only person left in the world.

'Well, I went forward, just putting a foot

at a time and it not leaving the ground, and at last I knew I was on the turf bridge. I tried not to think of the black oozy clabar below me on either side that would suck me in and close my eyes and stop my mouth. I was on all fours now, putting out my hands this side and that at the edge of safety, and then, being fairly sure of myself, I stretched down on the left – solid ground; down on the right – nothing. And I couldn't stop. I was away to bloody hell. My body tipped. I grabbed at nothing. I let out a scream. It's a wonder you didn't hear me ten miles away. Then the God of Mercy hit me on the head and I was nowhere.'

'Well,' said Andrew, 'if you had always brought the empty bag back to the post office you would have been sooner missed. Them silly torches. If the thing goes out, then you're worse than you never had it. Damn it all, man, when we found you, there you were with a small hole in your head, below the edge of a twelve-foot drop and nowhere near the bog, or the bridge that is in it, and the good doctor says it'll be a while before you're on the post again. Maybe Rab will be back from his holiday by then.'

'If I am for it again, indeed it will be three torches, and a bit candle and matches I'll be taking,' said Tommy, 'and I'll be keeping to the proper path.'

(Autumn 1965)

THE PARISH

Louisa Reid

'Meetin' at the 'all tonight? What meetin's that then? It bain't the W.I. for sure, nor the Mothers' Union, not on a Wednesday. They got the bus goin' to the dress show next week; I got me name down for that. Then there be the pantomime – Cinderella ain't it? There's a real nice show for the kiddies, bless their little 'appy faces. Lars' W.I. outin' was that there cinema into Yeovil. Real lovely that was. I could 'a' sat there an' seed it right on through again.

'What meetin' is it tonight then? Oh, the parish. No, I never goes to them now. There was a time back along I used to go, but now you 'as the same ol' ones sayin' the same things over, an' none of it don't get done, not to my knowledge it don't. Tell yer somethink about that parish council; they don't never get none o' the young 'uns goin' on it. They'm the ones what oughter be givin' up their evenin's to it. It concerns them more'n what it do us. It's their children what's growin' up into all this 'ere crime an' carry-on. Besides, it don't 'urt them a-turnin' out of a evenin'.

'Not that I mightn't go up along to the 'all if they was to 'old the meetin' in the summer like. But they always 'as it when the nights is dark. You got to leave the fire an' the telly an' go on with a torch, an' when you gets there, there ain't anyone 'ardly you knows. Anyways it's not the kind o' meetin' where you gets a chance of a talk to nobody. I mean, they'll go on from start to finish an' never stop for a cup o' tea an' a biscuit. Now bingo nights, that's different.

'You goin' to this meeting' tonight then?

Mebbe you'll like it all right if you never been afore. Lemme see now, what was they on about the lars' time I did go? Oh ah, it were postin' o' the letters. There was one lady wanted the 'oles in the letter boxes bigger 'n what they are, not them at the office but the little 'uns 'itched up in the 'edges down along the roads. Said as 'ow the envelopes is bigger now with all them forms you 'as to fill up. I ain't seen no difference since, so I reckon what she said didn't catch on.

'If you do go an' drains do crop up, if no one else don't mention it, would you mind to say they 'aven't never been yet to clear out that drain down along where you goes out o' my back gate? Ever since Christmas 'e've been like it an' it's not for want of askin'. An' that there wall down the road, 'e's bulgin' somethink dreadful. If any o' them big stones was to come out with the children passin' up to school, well. . . An' another thing. I reckon it be council's business to see we don't 'ave them dogs strayin' round o' nights. Come nosin' round my place knockin' the lids off the bins wi' a clatter to wake the dead. Oh ah, I knows well enough 'oo's they be, but it ain't for me to name no names. Come back to you, it do, an' there's no call for to go out o' your ways to make trouble.

'You wasn't 'ere for the votin', was yer? Up to school they 'ad it. No, I'm wrong there; that there was the rural. I don't never remember votin' for the parish. Anyways, it d' seem as most of 'em 'ave been on back as far as I remember. Well, I 'opes as 'ow you enjoys the meetin' an' they don't keep on too long. There's some of 'em 'as to 'ave their say, an' there's no stoppin' of 'em till they 'ad it.'

(Winter 1967)

TAIL CORN

Welsh butcher to customer complaining of bony meat: 'Well, missus, you buy land, you buy stones; buy meat, you buy bones.'　　　　*(Autumn 1970)*

Verger in Dartmoor church, to visitor admiring the large carved bosses on the oaken altar rails: 'Don't 'ee touch they there knobs, they be 'oly knobs. Bishop be short-sighted, an' when 'er were 'ere last time, 'er confirmed two o' they.'　　*(Winter 1950)*

Devonshire blacksmith, to old man who has brought a young horse to be shod: ''E 'aven't been shod before, 'ave 'e?' Old man: ''E 'aven't been shod afore before but 'e 'ave been shod be'ind before.'　　*(Winter 1947)*

Dalesman's criticism of uninspired performance by competitor at last year's Wharfedale Music Festival: 'Nobbut like a yard o' pump-watter.'　　*(Spring 1969)*

Old tithe barn in Sussex. (G. Pennethorne)

ON THE OLD FARM

HAND-PICKED HOP HARVEST

Geoffrey Guise

We were not to know, but this was to be the last year at Moore's Farm in Worcestershire that hop-picking would be done by hand into cribs. After this year – 1951 – the machines would take over completely.

There was a strict tradition that people from the same Staffordshire and Black Country towns and villages always picked at the same farm or parish in the country. For generations Shelsley Beauchamp, on the River Teme a few miles north-west of Worcester, had welcomed families from Tipton Green, Dudley, Brierley Hill and Pensnett Chase.

Recruitment of pickers was in the hands of older women from the towns, who were called 'takers'. To judge from their dark coiled hair and gold-hooped ear-rings, many of them had a background as gypsies or as canal boatwomen. They were paid very proper respect. The railways still ruled and special hop-picking trains of enormous length left Birmingham, calling at pre-arranged halts and stations. 'As long as a hop-picking train' was a common Black Country expression then.

Families began to pack their 'hopping boxes' weeks in advance. A common type was the Birmingham tin trunk, enamelled to look like grained wood. Sometimes, if the man of the household was something of a carpenter, the boxes were really of wood and became in the nature of heirlooms, treasured by successive generations. The boxes were consigned by rail well in advance of the annual migration. Regulars among the hop-pickers were the 'tatters', as the scrap-iron collectors of the city were called. They made hop-picking their annual holiday and travelled to the country by horse and cart or old lorry piled high with household gear, prams and offspring. Many sensible head-teachers turned a blind eye to the children's absences knowing that the annual break did them nothing but good.

Our party – two families with six assorted children between us – went down in John's old Austin with groaning springs and a boiling radiator. We were to meet the rest of the pickers at Mr Lionel Moore's fruit and hop farm. In those days the Shelsleys displayed an overwhelming impression of good and careful husbandry as we coasted down the long hill to the fields of soft fruit: the biggest cherry-trees we had ever seen, the damsons everywhere including the hedgerows, acres of every kind of English apple, ubiquitous yellow egg-plums and red Victorias.

'Mr Lionel', head of the Moore family, greeted many of the pickers by name. He was a well-loved and kindly man who paid particular attention to the welfare of the small children. Then began the allocation of barns and dormitory buildings (usually empty winter stores). Many barns were occupied on a hereditary family basis by pickers well-known to the Moores.

Large iron medieval-looking fire-baskets

were supplied to each party. These had rudimentary brick chimneys and were known as 'devils' – perhaps an allusion to the devil's griddle and the origin of the word 'devilled' as a way of cooking meat. Most of the serious cooking was done quite late in the evening after work. Rabbits figured often and there was rough cider to drink.

Early next morning we all paraded in the great farmyard to be sorted out and given our tasks. John and I were given the day-rated jobs as pole-pullers. We were armed with long poles and when called by any of the pickers, we pulled down the last strands of hops from the wires. Between answering these calls a pair of pole-pullers could pick 'half an end house'. 'House' is the Midland term for the amount of hops picked to fill one crib. This greatly augmented our day-wage.

Three weeks – allowing for some rain – was about the maximum period for the hop harvest; but on this mixed-fruit farm picking of some sort went on all summer. The

Dried hops. (Jean Lyne)

picking itself was done in a time-honoured way. The crib was a triangular-sectioned canvas bag which was made on the farm during the winter. It measured 4ft across the top and about 10ft in length; its volume was sufficient to accommodate the work of four pickers. The hop-bines were pulled in great swathes from the wires and laid across the top of the crib, where they could be easily picked into it. The strict rule was that no twigs or leaves should go in with the hops, a rule enforced by a refusal to 'bushel', i.e. weigh, a 'dirty-crib'. Clean hops were bushelled and a check given for their value to be cashed later at whatever the taker and farmer had agreed.

It was quite common to see a baby gurgling happily amongst the bines at one end of the crib and even making infant efforts at picking. The pickers were usually women and girls of all ages from seventy plus down to comely wenches, and singing seemed to be the happy habit of them all. Most of the Black Country husbands stayed at home during the family's hop-picking holidays because their factory holidays did not fit the harvest. This meant that many of the women and girls were unaccompanied, but there was no question of attentions being forced upon them. The older women were vigilant – but they could not always prevent the young and single ones from 'courting' on those wonderful summer evenings. Some of them would go into Worcester on a single-decker country bus to a Saturday night dance or a pub. There were many rescue calls from young couples stranded after missing the last bus back. Usually an old van or car set off at midnight to pick up the errant pair.

The free-and-easy life of the hop-fields in the best part of the year attracted strange characters, many of whom appeared regularly at the same time each year with no indication of where they had spent the intervening months – and no one asked. Some were disreputable but the strict behaviour code of the hop-yard and foremen kept them in line, apart from petty drunkenness on scrumpy.

The hop-fields contained all sorts and classes of people: hymn-singing old ladies, pop-of-the-day-singing girls and boys, tramps of the old school, rootless ex-servicemen whose wartime marriages had been broken, mystery couples with cultured backgrounds who lived in sin; and gypsies, a race apart and still with decorated horse-drawn caravans occupying their hereditary pitches. But the bulk were always decent Black Country folk, most of whom lived in council houses, but whose grandparents and great grandparents had been, not so very long ago, part of this rural scene and economy.

(Autumn 1984)

A HILL-FARMER LOOKS BACK

F. W. Brocklehurst

When I was a boy most of the farms in the limestone uplands of central Derbyshire varied between fifty and seventy acres, and money was scarce. I left school in 1904 at the age of thirteen, and my father then took on more land adjoining ours, making the total up to seventy acres. Four years later, when my brother left school, the Duke of Devonshire's agent divided up other land; we then had about 150 acres in all and a new set of buildings.

Most of the cattle were Shorthorns, and all the milking was done by hand. In summer the cows were milked in the fields. However much they swung their tails and kept moving because of flies or gnats, it was no use losing one's temper; otherwise one man's job became a task for two or three until the cow had quietened down again. The worst time for outside milking was when it was wet and windy and the three-legged stool sank into the ground. If the cow moved at all, it was quite a job getting up, lifting the stool and sitting down again. Also the rain ran off the cow's back on to our knees and forearms, so that we usually had to change our clothes when we had finished.

I did some recording, weighing milk, corn and hay to see how much profit there was from a good cow; but when buying a bull, one never knew if he had good milking blood in his veins. Many diseases now easily cured or prevented were serious then; milk fever, for example, was often fatal. I remember my father and uncle sitting up all night with one of grandfather's cows. They had given it half a bottle of whisky and piled hay and rugs on it to get a sweat; and the cow recovered. They were great believers in hot beer and whisky for all sorts of chills and were probably not far wrong. All calves were given two gallons of milk a day and kept until they were about a month old; they made good veal.

Cheese-making, which started about the middle of April, was the main source of income. Two farmers would join to make the larger cheeses in big pans, each holding about forty gallons. The milk was carried from the fields on yokes, perhaps with another can held in front, for distances of up to a mile. Some was heated on the fire to bring it all to a certain temperature, and rennet or part of a calf's stomach would be added before the pan was covered and left to turn. When the milk had curdled, mother would use first her arm and then a wooden bowl to break it down and divide the whey from the curd, which she pressed to the bottom of the pan, while taking off the whey. Next she cut up the curd and put it in a cloth under a small press to extract more whey. After dinner it was taken out, put in a pancheon and crimmed, or worked with the hands, salt being added and thoroughly mixed in. It was then put into a cheese vat, fitted inside with a tin garth that could go down as weight was added. After a day or two in a large press, consisting of a big square stone fitted on to a screw and fixed in a frame, it was put in a drying-room. Even in those days there was much foreign competition. I remember father being away all day with a load of cheese in the cart and returning without having sold any. I believe the highest price offered was 4d. a pound. Cheese making finished about September; then any milk left over, after the calves had

The farmhouse at Sheldon, near Matlock.
(William Scully)

been fed, the house supplied and a little sold retail, was 'set up' in pancheons on the pantry bench for butter. The skim milk was fed to pigs or calves.

Shortly after I left school we started to send milk to Manchester. Although prices were low, I remember how pleased father and mother were to receive a milk cheque every fortnight instead of waiting three months for the cheeses to ripen. Milk was sold at so much a dozen quarts – 1s. 6d. in summer and 2s. 6d. in winter – in those days. We took ours to the station every morning with horse and float, leaving the farm at 8.05 to catch the milk train at Longstone station, some three miles away, at 8.40. When the weather became warm in May we had to take it to Bakewell station every night, in case it went sour before being sold; we also took it there every Saturday night through the winter, so that there would be more for delivery on Sunday morning. There used to be some bad journeys in winter, two horses might have to pull the float through snow-drifts back up the dale, where gradients of one in six are common. On foggy nights the horse had to be left to find its own way back, because the candles in the lamps did not light very far. The farmer provided the churns, and when some of the bigger firms were overdone with milk, they would return none for several days. This continued until the Milk Marketing Board came into being many years later.

Prices remained much the same for a long time before 1914, when a good calving cow made about £20. The best cow father ever had was a red one which he took to Bakewell market. All the stalls were full, and we stood with her on the corner of what was Mr Sim's shop. There were quite a number of dealers who liked to buy a good cow, and we soon had customers about. The first bid came from a sharp little man in

The village street. (William Scully)

a bowler hat whose wife went everywhere with him, carrying a little bag of golden sovereigns to pay for any cattle bought. He would keep coming back to make what he stated in a most emphatic manner to be his last bid, and then walk away; but he never went quite far enough to let in another dealer who was waiting in the offing. This continued for quite a while, and eventually the cow went for £25 – a very big price at the time. Everything was sold privately in those days, either on the farm or at market. This started early, the cattle stalls being filled by 8 a.m.; father was usually home for dinner.

We kept a few sheep, selling most of the lambs but retaining a few ewe lambs to keep up the flock. For many years we bought a well-bred Lincoln ram and sold the ram lambs for stock purposes. This way they made a higher price than for fat, besides being something in which you could take more pride. They were usually coloured brown with umber and oil, which were put on the outside of the wool and

'Everyone kept Lincoln Longwools in those days.'
(William Scully)

squeezed in. These ram lambs were taken round to the various autumn fairs, fetching £3 or £3 10s. each instead of £2 or less for fat. Everyone kept Lincoln Longwools in those days. I remember later cutting 27 lb of wool from a tup, while the ewes averaged 14 lb.

We usually kept a sow or two and fattened one, after perhaps two litters, to kill in the autumn. As they were fed on maize meal and bran, the back fat was about 5 in thick, going down a long way before there was any sign of lean. It was quite an event when the pig was killed. There was a pig killer in the village, and he would come down about two o'clock and with extra help to hold it, stick the pig, some of the blood being caught to make black puddings. Meanwhile water had been boiled to scald off the bristles. Afterwards the pig was hung up, and the liver, kidneys, heart and so on were removed, to be divided among relations, who would in turn send us a share when they killed a pig. The pork also was cut out and divided up in the same way. The following day the rest of the carcass would be put in salt, with brown sugar and saltpetre added; it was usually rubbed till moist, so that the salt would penetrate

better. The charge for killing and cutting up was half a crown – quite a nice sideline at that time.

When I was nine or ten years of age we started to keep more poultry. Father bought boxes, took them to pieces and made hen-cotes from them. These were placed under stone walls in corners of fields, where they got most shelter from the winds. Only one was put in a two- or three-acre field, so that the hens could balance their own rations, as they were fed almost entirely on whole maize and a few home-grown oats. Most were Plymouth Rocks, Blue Andalusians, Leghorns and Wyandottes. Several farmers would send away for a sitting of eggs every year and, if these turned out well, others would buy cockerels to cross with their hens. We usually crossed alternately with light and heavy breeds and, though we got a variety of colours in the pullets, the results were quite good. We used to look in the cotes each morning to see which hens were laying, and if we saw one on the nest for several days in succession, we would save that bird for breeding. We kept strict accounts and found that, with no charge for labour, each hen made a profit of 5s. For many years we sent eggs to the Farnworth and Rearsby Co-operative Society, a number of farmers in the village bringing them to our house for packing; we received a shilling a box for our trouble. We spent some very interesting evenings packing eggs, while farming, politics, religion and all sorts of subjects were discussed.

Uncle John and family, father and ourselves used to join for haymaking; our meadows were close to his, so that it was not much trouble to go from one to another. Father did the mowing and hacked the wall-sides, pitched the hay, stacked and so on, while we children raked the backswath for the mower, tedded round the walls and turned most of the swaths, stopping now and then at corners to count the blisters. Uncle John's sixteen acres were divided into thirteen fields, so there were plenty of wall-sides and corners.

All the farm children worked hard in the hay and usually enjoyed it. We had rides in carts and good feeds in the open, though we often got blisters on our feet carrying the food and drink from home. The carts had shelvings but no gormers (end-pieces) to hold the hay on, and we learned at an early age how to build a load that would carry. All loading was done by hand, without forks, the hay being rolled into a sort of ball and built like bricks. This made it easier to unload because, if the hay was long, much pulling and tugging was avoided if the thrower-off knew just which place to form-off next.

Much of our seventy acres was moorland, but father had reclaimed twelve acres soon after he started to farm. This was our chief arable field, growing seeds, corn and roots. We used no artificial manures, but a lot of fields were limed, and sometimes ground bones or slag were applied. We did not like the ground bones, as they were not steamed or sterilised and it was thought they brought disease. All the oats were broadcast. We used to harrow once beforehand to prevent the loss of any seed between the furrows, and two or three times afterwards. We usually sowed eighteen stones to the acre, though some farmers sowed twenty-four stones. I used to sow an acre in three-quarters of an hour. Small grass seeds were sown with two fingers and the thumb, taking two yards as a cast and sowing with the wind, changing hands each way; this took about an hour per acre. Later, sowing with a fiddle drill, doing four yards at a cast as for oats, took about half an hour per acre.

Until I left school our few acres of oats

Broadcasting oats. (William Scully)

were all cut by scythe. When they were ripe father would cut a swath across a piece, the direction depending on which way the straw fell straight. It was then taken up by hand and, if the straw was long enough, he would pull out of the end of the sheaf a few straws with which to tie it; otherwise a band was made by twisting the heads of a few straws together. My first job, after raking clean with a hand-rake, was to make bands till father had finished mowing. Then he would take the corn up and lay it on the bands while I tied the sheaves. When stacking we always put five sheaves each side for a kiver, and two upside down on top for protection, tying them together to hold them firm. Two kivers we called a thrave, and the usual contract price for stacking was 3d. a thrave. If there was a bit of weed, twitch or clover in the bottom, two cuts of the scythe made two pick-ups from the swath and a sheaf. A fast worker could do a thrave in a quarter of an hour. Later we cut with a mowing machine with reaping attachment, leaving the corn in small heaps ready for

Oat harvest. (Geoffrey N. Wright)

tying up. We always counted how many thraves we had done, so that when a man who helped us went to the Devonshire Arms for a drink, he could brag a bit about it. He would give a preliminary cough and say, 'We cut so and so today'. 'You never did!' was then echoed all round. There was quite a lot of jealousy about finishing first on farms, though at that time those who did so usually went to help others.

Our corn stacks were always round, with three or four wagonloads in each. They were thatched up – a job I used to like because it was one in which you could take a pride. Nothing makes a farm look tidier than a lot of hay and corn stacks all well thatched; and on Sheldon Moor, if they had not been, they would have been blown all over the field. We never had a threshing machine. In winter each stack was taken to a loft as required. There we used to knock the sheaves three times on each side of a big barrel which stood in a corner, before throwing them down to the cows below. The oats from the barrel were fed to poultry or put through a winnowing machine and sacked up for seed.

We did not grow wheat or mangolds, because of the short summer and type of soil, but swedes and turnips could be heavy crops; I have known a root to weigh up to 14 lb. Nor did we grow many potatoes – just a few rows for the house and some bags for neighbours.

Farm wages were usually paid by the year, with one week's holiday from

Christmas Day till New Year's Day. About £20 a year was the average wage for a man living in. I remember how, when two next door got £26 a year, the old farmers said they were very good men. Overtime in the hay and corn harvests was all included in the year's wage, and the only time off was perhaps on Saturday afternoon, to watch or play cricket.

Most farmers had an Irishman for a month at least during hay harvest. They usually came over from Ireland to help with the hay in Lancashire, and then Derbyshire, before going on to Lincolnshire for the corn and potato harvest. Some came to the same farms year after year – one man for forty years – and they always brought their scythes with them. They were each paid £1 a week and keep, including drink in the hayfield, and a bed was usually provided in loft or barn. Most of them were good workers and in a big hurry to get the hay in while the weather was good.

On the land which we took over when I left school father showed me walls that had been built by his grandfather. They were about 5 ft high and looked like standing for another hundred years. One year father and Uncle John built a shed for six stirks with a barn on the end of it for hay. It was a lean-to shed with zinc roof, boskin and hay cratch. Father and uncle did the walling, and a cousin and I mixed the mortar and carried the stones. The village carpenter did the woodwork and the roof, and the total cost was £33. The wage of my cousin and myself worked out at 3d. an hour, and father's and uncle's at twice that. The wood, roof and carpenter's work cost £11 in all. It was as cheap a building as could be put up.

Father liked trees about the farm, and soon after taking on the additional land we had planted sycamores in the corners of the fields. They are now more than fifty years old and give shade and shelter; they also improve the looks of the countryside.

In those days in our village of Sheldon everyone knew everyone else's business. One person's sorrows were felt by all; and if a poor man's cow died there would be a collection for him. We were like one big family.

(Winter 1961)

HAYMAKING

Where once the haycocks lay
Soft-mounded and sweet,
Compounded was that hay
Of sorrel and cow-wheat,
Trefoil and tormentil,
Potentilla, meadowsweet,
Melilot and storksbill
Pungent in June heat;
Lady's bedstraw, woodruff,
Lady's mantle, marguerite,
With marjoram flowers enough
To make the air sweet;

Wagwants and nameless grasses,
Goosegrass, cocksfeet,
Feverfew and creeping Jenny,
Eyebright neat.

Where once the wagon rolled
Hoop-raved and proud
Across the shorn wold
Under the June cloud,
With slow sound of horse and wheel
Through aisles of grass and vetch,
Meadow-vetchling, self-heal,

The hay sweep, Yorkshire Dales. (Ron & Lucie Hinton)

The scented load to fetch –
Knapweed, silverweed,
Hawkweed and clover,
Meadow sage, meadow rue
The pasture over:
Meadow fescue, millet grass,
Timothy and rye,
Salad burnet, creeping cinquefoil
Under the June sky –

Now the stinking engine roars
Down streamlined fields.
Oblong hayblocks
Its vomit yields.
Of sterile and purest ley,
Parcelled and hard,
Compounded is that hay,
By no flower marred;
Tested and scentless,
Weedless and clean,
Clinical bales

Litter the June scene.

Yet when the summer moon
Rises over the wood
They are like standing stones
That have always stood;

Primeval and high,
Ageless, stark.
Their long shadows lie
In the June dark.
Older than haycocks
These cromlechs stand;
Immemorial
They rise from the land.

Man's strange ways,
Newfangled and odd,
Are all one
To the June god.
                    Robin Tanner (Summer 1961)

Haystacks. (Roy Dixon)

BLESSING THE GRAIN

Mildred Robertson

Fifty years ago I used to watch my grandfather and his workers on our Devon farm as they threshed out seed wheat with flails on the barn floor, then spread it evenly and dressed it with blue-stone (sulphate of copper) against the rooks, turning it over with long-handled spades until the dressing was evenly mixed. Next Grandfather piled all the wheat into one conical heap and, standing at each point of the compass in turn, placed his finger-tips together and pressed both hands sideways into the grain, making the marks of a cloven hoof in four rows from floor level to the top of the heap. Then, facing the east, he smote strongly with the handle of the flail on the top of the pile, and smote again from the south, to make the sign of the cross. If the grain so displaced obliterated the marks of the hoofs, the crop would be a good one. I can still see in my mind's eye the golden gleam of the wheaten straw standing in yealms ready for thatching, and feel the scratch of the starched lace of my pinafore under my chin as I sat on Grandfather's coat and watched the ancient custom.   *(Winter 1967)*

A VICTORIAN FARMER AND HIS MEN

Jean B. D. Radford

'I was told I had the first Chance at Mrs Bateman's Farm if she left it this year,' wrote Samuel Hirst, West Riding farmer and land valuer, on 1 January 1831, thus beginning the first of the fifty volumes of 'Dunn's Daily Remembrancer' that he was to fill before his death in 1880. He was born on 10 October 1803, and before 1831 he had been living with his elder brother William on the family farm at Stubbs Walden between Doncaster and Pontefract. He was now about to start farming on his own, for in February Mrs Bateman's farm, 313 acres at Kellington, did indeed become his at a rent of £480 per annum – 'and I hope to have many a happy Year to come at this place'. He was to remain there for the rest of his days.

Kellington is a low-lying area of light sandy loam situated in a fork formed by the river Aire and the Aire and Calder canal, about ten miles from Goole. It was noted, according to a nineteenth-century directory, for turnips and potatoes and its excellent quality of malting barley; and the latter crop, combined with sheep rearing, was Samuel's main source of farming income. Over the years this enterprise was expanded by 387 acres of land, so that at the time of his death he was one of the two principal landowners in the district. His obituary in the *Leeds Mercury* noted besides that 'as a land valuer in the farming interest his name is familiar all over England'.

Although his diaries contain a mass of fascinating minutiae about the people around him and events in his neighbourhood, the bulk of Samuel Hirst's daily jottings concern his farming, and one sub-ject he had plenty to write about was his labour force. He usually employed three or four 'farm servants' who lived in the farmhouse or, in later years, with the foreman. They were hired as a rule at Martinmas for a year, at the 'statutes' or hiring fairs at Pontefract or Snaith, at a wage from which they received odd advances, the balance being paid the following Martinmas. The farm servant was generally expected 'to wash for himself', and he received no holiday except on the day of the hiring fair and at Christmas, with an occasional day's leave for which he had to ask and which was sometimes refused him. Wages in the 1830s averaged about £6 a year for a boy and £12 for a man, rates that had roughly doubled by the 1870s. Maidservants received similar treatment and less money.

The rest of the farm labourers, of whom there were at least twenty-two by 1874, were paid by the week at a daily rate for six full days' work. Usually no payment was made during sickness: 'Paid Russett his wage up to this night, £22, not quite 9s. per week, he was ill a few weeks so I deducted £1 8s. off £23 8s. which leaves £22.' But there were exceptions: 'I paid Joe Stacey his wage for 2½ days lame.' There were one or two occasions when the men were paid for leave of absence: 'I paid all my men for this week although they went to the [Agricultural] show [at Selby] yesterday at 10 o'clock in the forenoon;' but those were obviously unusual in that they were specially noted. The weekly pay for day labourers in 1831 was 12s. This figure fluctuated, the lowest recorded being 10s. in 1851, and the highest 18s. in 1873. When the reduction to 10s. was made in December 1851 the men understandably

(W. T. Usher)

THE GATE

I like a five-barred gate.
I like its presence
between the shivering acres of the
   wheat
and this prosaic
meadowland of cattle.
It wears the marks of children's
   swinging feet,
and leans a little –
yet the catch is sure:
does not divide the lost from the élite

but is to both (and everyman) a door
into new territory.
So, it seems
to hang between reality and dreams,
a bond to both,
calm, practical, and knowing
the pattern of our various journeys
   here,
the pause,
the mingled shadows of our going.
        Jean Kenward (Autumn 1981)

complained, but all they got was a dusty answer: 'I told them those that did not come on Monday I should know did not want to work.' The following December they tried again: 'My men wanted a little more wage tonight, I said wait till 1 January 1853,' and an increase to 12s. was given on 7 January. A year later they were

receiving 15s. a week, but after three more years they were back to 13s., which Samuel appears to have considered ample. *25th September 1857:* 'I have let Thomas Backhouse have £1 towards his turnip seed. He is always in want of money, good wages but never no better.'

By the standards of his day Samuel Hirst

Samuel Hirst's red-brick farmhouse completed in April 1832. (Alec Wright)

does not seem to have been an exceptionally hard master, for several of his day labourers – Tom Backhouse among them – remained in his employ throughout the period of the diaries; and his foreman George Jordan, first engaged in 1840, was left an annuity in his will. There are not many instances of male farm servants absconding before their year's contracts had elapsed, and this would imply that conditions at Kellington were at least bearable.

Samuel and his wife, in their turn, were appreciative of loyal service, a point well illustrated by the grief expressed in the diaries when the deaths of two of their men were recorded. One of these was William Russett, already mentioned. His health began to fail on 13 March 1844, and the progress of his illness is noted almost daily between that date and his death on 26 May,

when we learn that 'Poor Russett, a faithful servant to me, and one who did everything in his power to please his mistress, departed this life about ½ past 12 o'clock this day, aged 50 years, may God Almighty have mercy on his soul.' Similar sorrow was felt when one Sam Stacey died. *2nd November 1861:* 'Sam Stacey a deal worse tonight, sent for another Dr Bywater.' *Sunday, 3rd November:* 'Mrs Hirst not at Church, she was at home weeping for the death of poor Sam Stacey, our old labourer which had worked for us 26 years, and he died this morning at 6 a.m. Oh that his end may be peace.' *4th November:* 'We have buried our poor old labourer, Sam Stacey, aged 56 years, we both followed him to his grave.'

There are many little examples of the Hirst's kindness towards their employees. 'I told the Doctor to lay out 20s. on Thomas

Backhouse.' 'Mrs Hirst gave her two girls a Bride cake betwixt them, two of them got wedd today.' 'I paid Ann Lockwood and Jont's wife 6d. each for being good company in Harvest;' that was in 1845, by which time he had mellowed a bit since July 1831 when 'Polly Russett left me because I told her to make less noise in the field'. 'I gave Tom and Bill Jordan [two of the foreman's sons] 2s. 6d. each to go to Leeds as they always wait nicely upon me.' There were occasions for jollity too, notably when the harvest was over. 'We have danced the Harvest this night. "Home" the Boys shouted merrily. Mrs Hirst and I stood by the garden gate to hear them come from Top Mill Close.' Afterwards a supper would be given for the men: 'All went home at 8 o'clock.'

At the same time Samuel Hirst expected value for money. 'Told my labourers that they were to get their Breakfast at home and not in the fields' – not that is, in working hours. 'I told the men that 38 loads manure is not a day's work for 6 men and 6 horses.' 'I went to Low Common after dinner and found the men not at work at 1.45, gave them a good blowing up.' One assumes that a tongue-lashing was preferred to the corporal punishment he was apt to mete out when roused to wrath: 'I gave Jack a good flogging.' Sometimes he does not even give the reason, but on that occasion there had been 'some very nasty talk' with the milkmaid. 'I pulled Thomas Backhouse his ears pretty soundly.' 'I gave James Backhouse a dressing with my whip tonight for going down the town without my leave'; two years later, 'James Backhouse left me today because I whipped him for sauce.' 'I gave Dick a good dressing with my stick.'

The farm servants were expected to keep regular hours, and even on Sundays they seem to have had to observe a fairly early curfew. 'Our lads have been out after they have got their Drinking [the refreshment provided at the farmhouse] till after 8 o'clock and I took the Lanthorn out for them and told them not to play that trick again.' 'Two boys went without Drinkings because they were not in by 6 o'clock.' 'Jonathan and Frank not at home this afternoon, taken away without leave, so next Sunday I must ask them where I shall have to send to if I want them.' How the poor fellows amused themselves during the long evenings they were expected to spend in the house is never revealed.

Lateness or absence without leave sometimes resulted in dismissal. *Sunday, 10th April 1842:* 'Bill Shooter did not go to Church today when I gave him orders to go, so I shall let him go.' *11th April:* 'Paid Bill Shooter his wage for the time he had been (because he was out last night).' 'Ab. Lund left us today for leaving home yesterday.' 'Lockwood has left me because I found fault with him for coming late for dinner.' 'Ed Farrer could not get to his horses till nearly 9 o'clock this morning, so he must go in the morning and work somewhere else.'

Dishonesty, disobedience and the use of bad language were also unforgivable sins. 'Nathan Wright pocketed 4 eggs, so I paid him his wage 8s. and turned him off.' 'Mrs Hirst found her maid out in removing a Bottle out of the Shoeplace. She must leave.' 'I turned Henry Gothard away this day for not doing what I ordered.' 'Turned Charles Stacey off for abuse to Pea Pullers.' 'Ordered Jack Bamforth to be sent home this morning for not obeying Geo. Jordan's orders.' Jack Bamforth's wife also got into trouble when she 'would go home in a hurry last night so I told Jack whatever they wanted it would be 6 o'clock before she could leave her work so she came crying to ask to be forgiven'. On one occasion, 'Cowman began beating a Cow and Mrs

Hirst spoke to him and he swore at her, so he shall go away, I won't have him.' Joe Stacey, who seems to have been accident-prone, having at different times had two mishaps when ploughing, broken 106 eggs in one go on his way to market and cut his foot while digging a drain, all without a harsh word being recorded even if said, was sacked in 1873 'because he was saucy last night'.

THE GROWER

The texture of soft berries, he knows
    them each from each –
The glossy gleam of apple-skin, the
    velvet touch of peach.
How sweet they come, the pear and
    plum
That hang within his reach.

Uncertainty and hope fill all the
    grower's hours,
Knowing the need at different times,
    for sunshine or for showers,
Counting the cost when hail or frost
Threatens his fruit and flowers.

But like his fruit he grows a skin
    protecting from the storm
And like his flowers he lifts a face for
    morning sun to warm
And, would-be wise, he never buys
Strong drink in any form.

He raises neither grapes nor hops, his
    credo to uphold.
'Buy land, not poison, is my aim. A rich
    man when I'm old!'
Thus he aspires while he acquires
That slower poison, gold.
Coral Copping (Autumn 1983)

Maidservants presented different problems. Mrs Hirst's standards must have been too high for most of the local lasses, judging by the number who 'didn't suit' and were sent packing almost as soon as they had arrived. *1835:* 'New girl came to her place today, Mrs Hirst wishes she had never seen her, sadly out of tune about the girl, but I hope my good Lady will get better.' Mrs Hirst's forebodings were justified though, for we learn that twelve days later she was dismissed for having stopped out all night after attending a wedding. *1841:* 'New lass came to her place, but Mrs Hirst says she won't do so she went and hired another and she must go.' *1842:* 'Mrs Hirst's girl won't suit her I am sure, so she is to leave.' *1846:* 'Ann Foulstone left us this day, not fit for our place.' Several appear to have had reciprocal sentiments about their mistress, for they either had second thoughts after hiring and did not turn up at Kellington at all, or they ran away, leaving their godspennies on the table. One was hauled back by her father – 'but we won't have her'.

Those who stayed were occasionally allowed visitors. 'Mrs Hirst not at Church today because we had our Maiden's sister to see her and they might have looked the House over.' To have sat through the sermon, which Samuel often found over-long – 'rather Ranting-like I call it' – imagining two giggling girls trying on all her bonnets, was evidently too much.

Of course, other difficulties arose. *27th February 1842:* 'Mrs Hirst's head maid [Sarah Sharp] has taken a great liking to our Lad not a man, and I have told him that if he cannot attend at my hours to his work he shall leave the next time he is behind time. Mrs Hirst told her maid that if she was her she would have a man, not a boy, to run after her. When Ladies get rather into years they will take anything in the shape of

Kellington Church: the Hirsts supported it and the chapel generously. (Alec Wright)

a man rather than be without a Lover. Very soft of them to do so, but I suppose they cannot help it, poor things.' *1st March:* 'Our girl very cross about her Lover going to leave. I won't keep two in a House that are sweethearts.' *18th March:* 'Mrs Hirst told Sarah she was to leave.' In 1845, 'I have told Bessy that I don't like to wait on myself and let her go without leave with Boys in the Town.' And sometimes the worst happened: 'Our kitchen-maid left last night and got her bed of a child same night.'

After all these strictures it is the more surprising to discover the tolerant attitude taken by both the Hirsts towards drunkenness among their workers. It seems that a man could almost reach a state of dipsomania before he would be dismissed; but one gathers from the diaries that over-indulgence in drink was almost a local pastime for rich and poor, male (including Samuel himself in his salad days) and female alike, so the vice was perhaps looked upon not with disgust but simply as a way of life. And because the sagacious horse could usually be relied on to find its own way home, a drunken groom was presumably less of a menace on the road than would be his twentieth-century counterpart. The Hirsts endured at least three bibulous grooms. *11th August 1838:* 'Oxley got drunk today at Market.' *Sunday, 12th August:* 'Our man Oxley been Drunk today again, and I collared him to make him go to bed and he said "Don't strike, master", so very good-humouredly that he made Mrs Hirst and self laugh at him.' *8th September:* 'Oxley came home Drunk again from

Market.' *Sunday, 9th September:* 'Oxley been home all day without leave, he must go in the morning.' *10th September:* 'I paid Tom Oxley his wage because he could not get home from Market.' *11th January 1840:* 'James got tipsy. I told him I did not think it very civil.' *16th February:* 'James gone home today, got Tipsy.' *17th February·* 'Gave James a good setting down.' *19th September:* 'Mrs Hirst went to Market and Rick Moxon drove her home because James got tipsy.' *13th January 1841:* 'When we got Home James was not there to take our Horse, so when he came I told him I should give him a month's warning to see out for a better place. I would not pay a man 14s. a week and take my own horse.' One of his successors was even worse. *31st July 1863:* 'Mrs Hirst gave William the Groom a good Blowing up for being Drunk.' *18th July 1864:* 'William full of drink and very cross, says he will leave in a month.' However, he stayed and his sprees continued throughout the next two years. So it is almost ludicrous to find that, in April 1867, he was instantly dis-

missed for 'stealing milk when the man came in with the milk'.

Drunkenness among farm workers is also noted from time to time in a similarly matter-of-fact manner. 'George Hall been home today and got Drunk I suppose.' 'Jont drunk or sleepy, could not do anything.' 'Hardy Jackson been drinking all day instead of working.' 'Lad got Drunk today at Stone-leading.' 'I think the Gardener has had too much to drink today.' 'I told the Gardener I would not allow Drinking as he has done of late.' 'Gardener been drinking all the afternoon, and his Brother been to seek him.' 'Priestley's wife and daughter both got Drunk today, and Priestley did not come this afternoon to work.' The examples are legion; but drunkenness is rarely given as the reason for dismissal, even when a habitual toper is sacked. Perhaps Samuel considered that those who had lived in glass houses were in no position to cast stones. It was no wonder that in 1878 an official named Mr Goodall 'came to see about drinking in this town'.

(Autumn 1966)

A STRIKE OF FARM WORKERS

In 1866, the following letter was received by Hannah, the young widow of Edward Tull, who was a descendant of the famous Jethro. It was from her

employees at Peasmore Farm, near Newbury. We received it from her great-granddaughter, Mrs Rita Perkins.

Peasmore April 18th *66*

Hon^d **– Madam**

We your Humble Servants take the liberty to adress you with a few lines on a *rather Painful Subject* which we will briefly lay

before you; your Petitioners his some of your *old Servants* mostly them, and we all are something like the *Israelslites* was in *Josephs* time; all was well until another *King* arose that knew them not. Then the task masters began to afflict them and so it as

(Robert Miller)

mornings and we told we would come if they would rise so when we went at 7 our usal time on Monday after waiting ¾ of a Hour Mr Chapmans Come to us and asked how it was we was not to time we told him we was so 2 or 3 of us as was wanted Particular was to go to work and the rest of us then said what are we to do, *when the* answer was you can go back and come for ¾ of a day. So we asked him if our wages was to be rose they said 9/- was suficient. So we said if one was to go back we all would for we was determin to have an alteration. We should have been the last to Strike had we been treated as men you been getting worse and worse ever since our *dear Mr Tull* has been took from among us. He used to stand up for us and we for him, some of us have, and are now, as have large families, nearly *starved*, and now are nearly – *naked*, and some of us have nothing to Plant our gardens with and cannot get it out of 9 *shillings* per *week* we *beg* to *Call* your attention to the Price of Provisions which are so dear and have been all the winter. Many of us with our *wifes* and 4 or 5 *Children* many times sit down to nothing but *Bread* and *water* and a few *Potatoes* in addition on a *Sunday*, and scarcely any *fire* to have it by =*Truly Madam* we may say our garden of *roses* as was once the *Pride* of *Berkshire*, now become a *Garden* of bitter *Herbs*= We have been asking for the advance of 1/- Per week for a long time but still the answer was *no*, and we are gone to Shop and had things until we are ashamed to go any longer=We was orderd to come at ½ past 6 o'clock

Sowing seed with a fiddle in Argyll. (H. E. Tyndale)

[105]

Honing a sickle near Rostrevor, Co. Down.
(Thomas McCleary)

Milking by hand. (D. J. Evans)

know that in the time of the rioting we all stood and gaurded the Place and our Dʳ Old Master said his men would Protect him and so we did and would again Could we get the Chance to do so Dʳ Madam fearing we have trespassᵈ to much on your Valuable time. Praying you to do something in our behalf, the Hired Servants was to have tablebeer but nothing to be had but Tankwater for *them* Robᵗ Bolton has been Carpentering & Whitewashing find tools and all for 9/- Per week and not a Drop of Beer. So these are a few of the Many Grievances and we wish we could send you a brighter Catalogue. Hoping and trusting your Ladyship his quite well and may *God bless you*, shall ever be our *Prayer*

[Sign d your Humble *Servants*]

Jacob Bolton	James Jones
Willᵐ Bolton	Geo Appleton
Isaac Bolton	John Taylor
Robᵗ Bolton	Geo Leek
James Hayes	James Culliman
James Smith	Geo Grace
Geo Hedges	Edward Jordan
Chas Grace	
Chas Bolton	P.S, I forgot to say
Geo Deadman	Mr Clarks men struck
Isaac Hamblin	at the same time

(Winter 1959)

Crackley Lane in Warwickshire. (W. J. Usher)

BEASTS OF THE FIELD

LONG AGO, MY BRIGHT DARLINGS
Anne Norrie

Above the gentle tilt of a green Suffolk valley stood a long, low, grey house with a garden enclosed by a thick holly-hedge, in which there was a gate opening into a steeply sloping meadow. The hedge was protected by a chain, stout fence-posts and bars. On these, most summer evenings, fifty years ago, I would hang, a youthful tomboy, waiting the arrival of the meadow's nightly tenants: three pairs of Suffolk Punches from the farm half-a-mile away in the village.

I would hear them clattering down the road; the leaders appeared at the meadow gate, the athletic young horseman astride the offside animal. There was the rattle of the spring latch on the gate, a tossing of maned heads, a clink of harness, then 'Giddy up, Jip' and the leaders, followed by the other two pairs (less spectacular, their riders favouring the traditional sideways seat of the farmworker) trotted, with the inimitable controlled freedom of the true Punch, on to the flat top of the meadow.

Off came the men and in one movement, as it seemed, off came the bridles. A friendly blow with the coiled reins on the rear of the notorious Jip sent the animals on their joyous gallop to freedom. Harness was dropped over the wire fence, a jacket, left since morning, picked up, and their feet scrunched wearily over the pebbles at the gate as the men passed out on to the road and went their several ways.

So the men went – but the horses! The horses thundered like the charge of an army, down over the green curve of the meadow as over the edge of the world. Down they galloped with power and grace and gladness to where the water bubbled up through the trough at the foot of the slope. How they drank – jostling each other, tossing their heads while droplets sparkled from their muzzles, or bending graceful necks to draw long draughts which could be heard from my fence. Then, turning from the trough, they rolled on the

(William S. Paton)

rich grass by the walnut-trees, great steel-shod hooves fully 6 ft in the air.

Then they would wander up the hill's green curve, grazing at will, their chestnut flanks gleaming like bronze in the evening sunlight. On the fence bar I would wait with flattened palm held out; on it a sugar lump or a piece of bread. Unhurriedly a huge form would approach and with enormous velvet muzzle gently take the proffered titbit; then stand munching, one hind hoof delicately tilted, long sandy eyelashes fringing kindly hazel eyes, magnificent blond tail engaged in dispersing the mourning choir of gnats. From the safety of the fence I dispensed more treats and caressed with delight proud necks and silken ears. Dusk came, and with it 'goodnight'; then, under the rising moon, the horses turned to graze near the old oak at the crest of the slope.

My window opened on that meadow and shortly after dawn, through mists of sleep, I would hear the squeaking of leather, the clinking of buckles and 'Giddy up, Jip'.

Those darlings of my young days! I scent their sweat, the sweetness of crushed grass, the cool tang of water and the summer's warmth rising in the evening air. I hear again their neighing, the snorts and puffs of eager breath; and over all the thunder of twenty-four hooves as they galloped over that curving meadow . . . the green field at the edge of the world.

(Summer 1984)

MEAL AND MUCK

Charles Batts

Jacky Painton was our pigman at Glebe Farm on a hill by the Berkshire Thames. He had worked for my father from boyhood. At fifty he could neither read nor write, but he had a rich store of earthy wisdom and an astonishing flow of language, and you could hear his laugh half a mile away. He also had a wooden leg.

One day he had been helping with the haymaking until seven in the evening and was hurrying back to the farm, for pig-feeding time was four o'clock. As he drew near the cries of his hungry pigs rose in crescendos of anguish. 'Wait a bit, yew idle varmints,' he chuckled. 'Wait a bit. I ain't 'ad me own grub yet. Me belly's as empty as yourn.' Puffing and blowing, the peak of his tattered old cap drooping over his right ear and the broken stump of a clay pipe hanging upside down from his mouth, he made for the barn, where he began to mix barley meal and water in a huge cobwebbed tub. "Oller away, yew pot-bellied little gutsers,' he muttered. "Oller away. If yew 'ad all as yew wanted yew'd bust yerselves an' the boss 'ud go broke.'

Filling two large buckets with the glutinous mass, he fitted a yoke to his shoulders and stumped off to his screaming charges. Tucked under his arm was the stick with which he stirred the meal – a useful and necessary weapon. The wet meal dribbled from it all down his trouser leg, but he did not mind. His corduroy breeches were stiff with the stuff and with other farm products collected over the years. Arriving at the first sty he put the buckets down outside, gave a twitch to his old cap, fixing it more firmly on his head, and spat with fervour into the palm of each hand. Then, gripping his stick, he lifted one bucket and slipped into the sty with a dexterity born of long practice, shouting at the black and white fiends who hurled themselves upon him screaming and jumping over each other, falling into and over the iron troughs, his stick whacking them wherever it happened to land.

'Get back, yew gre't galluses!' he shouted. 'Get back! Drat yer eyes an' limbs. Get yer gre't snouts outa the bucket. Damn an' blast the lot o' yew! 'Alf on the perishin' floor an' over me trousers. Take that, an' that!'

The eight heavy pigs left him in peace for a moment, grunting and guzzling as he slipped out for the other bucket; but as they saw him coming back they rushed madly towards him. Jacky went down before this fresh onslaught, falling across the broad back of a large black sow who tossed him, without ceremony, on to a white comrade with head stuck in the over-turned bucket. This white champion – Jacky's favourite, named Horace at birth – was in turn overwhelmed by his fellows, who clambered over him and their fallen keeper, splattering him from head to foot with meal and manure.

Alerted by the terrific clamour, I had been in time to witness Jacky's overthrow. He lay now with the thin end of his wooden leg stuck under one of the metal bars which divided the trough into sections, unable to get up and completely helpless. He was shouting, 'Mass'r Charles! Mass'r Charles! Come yere, 'ull 'ee? These yere devils 'ave a-got I down.'

I could not hurry for laughing and just stood there holding my sides. Jacky's face, hair and body were plastered with meal and muck. His pipe was gone, and his white favourite Horace, chewing his cherished cap and finding it too tough a morsel, was now trying earnestly to eject it. One of Jacky's arms was round Horace's fat neck, and he seemed to be gazing benevolently into the pig's face, but he was swearing fearfully, spitting out straw and dirt as he did so. Horace, squeaking angrily, shook his great head and the treasured cap fell and was trampled into the mire. This almost broke poor Jacky's heart. 'Fer Gawd's sake, Mass'r Charles,' he pleaded, 'do 'ee stop laughing' an' 'elp I up. Damn the 'ungry devils, they be trying to e't I alive. I be proper winded.'

As I stooped to help him, Horace blundered heavily against the trough and I heard a sharp crack. 'There's me ruddy leg gone west,' roared Jacky, 'as 'ull cost I thirty bob to get another, an' me cap all chewed by that ruddy 'Orace as I raised from a young 'un.'

I got him up and listened with fresh admiration while he damned all pigs, living and dead, to hell and beyond. 'Perishin' sons o' bitches they be! Look at the cap as I've 'ad fer twenty year! An' me weskit an' trousers mangled all to 'ell! Ah, yew can laugh, boss. An' me old pipe! Where is 'e? Billy Weston gie I that pipe at Abingdon Fair, fifteen year come Michaelmas time. I wouldn't 'ave lost 'e fer a week's pay. An' –,' clutching at my shoulder for support, ''ow be I goin' to get 'ome on one leg?'

'Don't worry, Jacky; I'll run you home,' I said.

'Thank 'ee, Mass'r Charles. Pick up me cap, will 'ee, afore they total ruins it.'

I handed him the filthy treasure. He looked at it sadly, shook it, slapped it once or twice against his thigh and stuck it on his wildly ruffled head, peak over one ear as usual. Then, as he looked at me, the old rascal burst out laughing and we roared together like happy schoolboys. After a moment I said, 'You're never going through the village with that awful rag on your head? Throw it away and I'll buy you another.'

'Thro' 'im away?' he protested. 'Not me. I'll take 'im along 'ome an' when me missus 'ave washed 'im an' put a stitch or two in 'im, 'e'll look like noo.' Then, as an afterthought, 'Me breeches be split to 'ell, an' I've only 'ad 'em ten years, mind yew. Mr Webb up at shop charged I seven an' a tanner for 'em. Extra spechul they wus. "Yew got a bargain," 'e said, an' 'e gie I a ounce o' Red Bell terbaccer fer luck.'

I promised Jacky full reparation. As he was hopping out of the sty, leaning on me, he stopped and with shining eyes fished his pipe out of a mass of filthy straw, wiped it on his dirty trousers and thrust it upside down in his mouth. 'That's better!' he said. 'I'd sooner 'ave lost a pound than 'im.'

After a good swill under the pump I drove Jacky home, sitting proud as a peacock beside me, puffing away at that dreadful pipe. The village carpenter worked a miracle with the broken leg. He bored a deep hole in the main block and inserted a piece of wood shaped like the leg of a Windsor chair. Jacky was right proud of that piece of craftsmanship and showed it to everyone he met. "E's most as good as 'e was afore, Mass'r Charles,' he told me next day, 'an' 'e only charged I two bob.' Then off he stumped, pipe upside down, ancient cap askew, whistling merrily, to see to his varmints.

(Winter 1966)

THE HORSE DOCTOR

John T. Cantlay

Minty died recently in his ninetieth year, and the parishes of Cruden and Slains in Aberdeenshire will miss his raw-boned gangling figure, always with a big black collie close at heel. He was by trade a slaughterman, which gave him his first insight into the anatomy of farm animals. He also acquired a long scar from elbow to wrist – the result of his contracting the dread disease of anthrax. The doctor saw little hope of recovery but did his best by cutting out the affected part and cauterising the wound with a red-hot iron. It was all done without anaesthetic, the patient being firmly tied down and given a bottle of whisky to suck.

When Minty married he rented a small farm and found that he had a gift for helping calving cows and lambing sheep. Neighbours were soon calling on him to assist with difficult cases. My earliest recollection of Minty is of seeing him stripped to the skin, sprawled in the 'greep' behind a cow, getting the calf into the proper position for delivery. He was very gentle, as many big men are, and his great strength permitted him to continue long after a lesser man would have had to give up.

He taught me how to 'drog' or give a bottle of medicine to any farm animal; and I was very proud when, under his tuition, I managed to administer a 'ball' to a horse. I had to insert my left hand into its mouth and pull the tongue well out. Then, holding the ball between the first and third fingers, with the second finger on top and the thumb and little finger tucked in below, I had to put my right hand into the horse's mouth well down by the grinders, still holding the tongue firmly. Then came Minty's master-stroke, which never failed. A little jerk of the right hand, and the ball slid forward; then the hand was quickly withdrawn, the tongue released, and a sharp slap instantly administered to the soft muzzle. This caused the horse to throw up its head in surprise and to swallow the ball. Minty had been groom to a vet and learnt something about animal medicines; he dispensed some rare concoctions, mixed with black treacle or linseed oil, and they usually worked.

When many cattle were sent from Ireland to be fattened off in our Aberdeenshire byres, where traditionally beasts are tied by the neck, they died like flies. Minty was called in and, saying 'It's jist the peemony, man', proceeded to administer his medicines, adding strong mustard plasters to the lung area. These brought tears to the eyes of man and beast, but many of the sick recovered. Minty advised that new arrivals be kept in the open for a while after their long and stifling journey by land, sea and land again from as far away as Co. Sligo. He was right; after a period in the fields the cattle could be tied up quite safely for fattening.

He never seemed to receive much money for his work; but loads of straw and swedes would often be seen going to his place. He did all the casualty slaughtering, getting the skins in payment; he was also kept busy killing pigs for home curing. Between the wars the dread 'grass sickness' in horses defeated even Minty. Then came penicillin, M. and B. and other modern drugs which made his doctoring unnecessary. He was still called in to calvings and lambings; but he was a little sad at being less in demand. His great physical strength was now declining and, though he still cycled from farm to farm, it was more for the sake of a gossip with neighbours than anything else. He must have been one of the last horse doctors, and farming will be the poorer for his passing.

(Summer 1962)

THE CULL

Old, lame, barren and at last dry
After a lifetime turning fields into milk.
She never knew her own loyalty. Her
   feet and jaws,
Two tools for grazing, worked
   unceasingly.

Still chewing she followed me
From the safe embrace of the herd,
Trust leading her like a halter to the
   lorry.
Then her contented wits flared into
   panic.

We must not give them human
   understanding,
They are unaware of treachery and
   profit –
Matters so peculiarly ours;
But I read in her eyes the question
   'Why?
I have paid half your bills these last ten
   years'.

Edward Stocker
(Spring 1987)

WORK WITH OXEN

George Ernest Holter, who lives at Seaford, was born at Exceat Farm. His eldest brother William, now eighty-seven, still lives there and works part-time on the farm. George was eleven years of age when he started work at Exceat Farm and, with a break for the 1914–18 war, he stayed there until 1925, when Edward Percival Gorringe sold the oxen along with the farm.

George's wife Kathleen writes:

'There were probably two reasons why oxen were used quite extensively: they were easier to train than horses – the ox is by nature a quiet, gentle, plodding creature – and cheaper to feed, making do with hay, oat straw and a little cotton cake and dried grain.

'In Sussex the teams were yoked in pairs, and a chain ran from the middle of the yoke to the pole or neb of the wagon. When an old pair was retired, a young one had to be trained. A yoke would be held by a wall and the young oxen driven forward until they put their heads through the bows of curved ash that acted as collars. The youngsters were placed in the centre of the team, with an experienced pair before and behind. The master ox of a team was placed on the off side, and the ox-herd called "Gee, Leader" for a left turn or "Hi, Lamb" for a right. If any persuasion was required, he used a 9 ft ash stick or goad having at its tip a sharpened nail of the regulation length of one barleycorn; but a word was usually sufficient and, when ploughing, a trained team would turn at the end of a furrow without command.

'What was known as a pickaxe team was used for extra heavy work, such as pulling an old Sussex wagon full of large (2¼ cwt) sacks of grain from the thresher to the farm. Six oxen were harnessed in the lead to set a steady pace and share the strain with four horses behind. Even with such a

A lift home for the girls from a Bishopstone team.

Timber hauling by oxen.

team the oxen often sank up to their knees in the soft ground, their tails stiffening with the effort.

'The oxen did not need blinkers; but when they worked in tempting surroundings they wore nets over their muzzles, for if one had bent its neck in stopping to graze, it would have hurt the neck of its yoked partner. Ox cues were sometimes found on the farm, but even my father-in-law, who was born more than a hundred years ago, could not remember an ox shod in his time.'

It seems that oxen were usually shod only when they had much work to do on flinty roads. Maude Robinson, writing in *A South Down Farm in the Sixties,* first published by Dent in 1938, described the process:

'The bovine intellect cannot be taught to lift one foot at a time to the blacksmith's knee, which is an early lesson for all horses. When a bullock was to be shod, it was thrown down on soft grass, the smallest ox-boy rushed in and sat on its massive neck to keep it from struggling, the four feet were bound to a tripod of poles, and the blacksmith nailed on the shoes at his leisure. Of course there were two "cues" to each foot, of rather thin iron, somewhat the shape of a comma. We always knew that bullock shoeing was in prospect when the blacksmith, Miles Mobsby, sent to ask for a piece of fat pork for a pincushion. The long sharp nails were stuck into this so that each was slightly greased. The great creature took this drastic treatment very calmly. When the ropes were untied, and the boy rolled off the neck, it rose slowly, gave a mighty shake and at once began to graze.'

In some countries or regions, where shoeing had to be done more regularly, a frame was built and the ox was hoisted from the ground by means of a broad canvas belt under the belly and some primitive form of windlass. James Keillor of Wading River, U.S.A., was told by a local farmer that a blinder, originally made for a savage bull, was occasionally used when a difficult ox had to be shod. One can only imagine that the unhappy animal had, at some time, been pricked by a badly inserted nail.

In Gloucestershire, Oxfordshire and Wiltshire collars were preferred to yokes. 'Oxen broke themselves to harness,' R. H. Wilson writes from Bishopstone Farm near Swindon. 'They were hitched to a baulk of timber and left in the yard. In three days they had learnt to pull.' J. R. Farmer of Filkins recalls: 'Wooden hames were used on horse and ox alike, but the ox hame has the "drawbar", the trace attachment, higher. The ox carried his neck flat, and the line of the pull was along his backbone, whereas a horse pushes with shoulder and hock. A horse would put his weight against a load and, if he could not get it rolling, might give up; but an ox would move forward step by step and shift a heavier load than a couple of horses. I remember

seeing the thresher coming to Oxlease: two horses pulled the engine, but the drum, which was heavier, was drawn by an ox, so slowly that you could hardly see it moving. The oxen were broken at eighteen months, worked two or three seasons and then, when the spring cultivations were done, fattened for Christmas. The meat was not so fat as some of the young stuff sold today. A great deal of their bulk was muscle put on at work.'

R. H. Wilson talked of the old days with Dick Chivers, the last man to work oxen on his Bishopstone farm:

'Because of the horns the collar was U-shaped. It was put on upside down, fastened with a strap and then twisted round till the buckle and strap were on top and the thickest part of the flocking rested on the brisket or chest. We used wooden hames; our carpenter always had plenty of spares, and a break could be repaired or replaced in minutes. We had iron hames, but they were used chiefly for horses on

Bathurst oxen, wearing 'spit and polish'. (M. Wight)

road work, as a form of spit and polish: they usually had a little brass knob on top and a brass plate where the tug chain was attached. We worked two teams, each of four oxen, from 1904 until 1921.

'My father's chief excuse for this somewhat eccentric link with the past was that they kept the arable cultivation up to date. They were never called upon for hay-making or harvest; but when the horses were busy with these, the arable work would have fallen very much behind, had it not been for the continuous ploughing by the bullocks. The custom had one drawback; they became very clock-conscious, and nothing would persuade them to do another stroke of work after three o'clock, their recognised time for knocking off, unless the last turn would be pointing for home. On one occasion we needed one more wagon for hay, and my brothers and I thought that, if they were allowed to come back home and have their meal, we might be able to kid them to turn out again. To our surprise, they offered no resistance, although it entailed two being fitted up with thill harness and put into the shafts of the wagon, a task they rarely encountered. All went well for a time, and we had nearly finished the load when they must suddenly have realised that they had been taken for a ride. At the far end of the field was a bridge spanning a considerable stream. Possibly urged on by the buzz of a gad-fly, off they went at full gallop, tails in the air, with myself and a brother on the top of the hay. The bullocks went under the bridge, but the load was too tall to follow them, so we jumped off into the stream. The bullocks remained in the shade, contentedly chewing the cud, until the cool of the evening, when we unhitched them and they walked quietly home, leaving the wagon and the load of hay.' *(Spring 1971)*

THE RELUCTANT EXECUTIONER
Mika Eumorfopoulos

There are those to whom a hen is simply an egg-producing machine, to be refuelled at regular intervals and discarded when worn out. Old Sam is not one of these. Left to himself he would, I think, establish a kind of home for aged and handicapped hens. 'Give the poor thing a chance,' he says, when I suggest despatching some sorry-looking bird. 'Once 'tis dead, 'tis dead': a statement I cannot deny.

A while ago a neighbour offered to look at my modest flock. Their bright eyes and brilliant scarlet combs filled me with pride, but the expert shook his head disparagingly. 'Culling,' he said, 'that's the secret of successful egg production, culling. I'll leave you these leaflets; they'll help you.' He trod on an egg, laid like an offering at his feet: 'You'll never make much profit this way,' he repeated.

I passed this information on to Sam next day with his elevenses. He looked up. 'Never reckoned to make much profit, did we?' he asked tersely between mouthfuls of bread and cheese.

'Well,' I said, 'I want to be able to pay your wages.'

'Wages!' he snorted. 'It don't take much profit to pay my wages.' This, alas, was true. He could earn half as much again at the poultry packing station and, as he had once hinted darkly, have some idea what time he would finish in the evening. But some incomprehensible loyalty makes him stick to me, or is it simply that he could not bear the sight of those endless swinging corpses? Feeling perhaps that he had been unnecessarily unkind, he added, 'What I'd like is to see you make a little over for yoursen.'

'That's nice of you, Sam,' I said, as I perused one of the leaflets. 'It says here that hens kept in batteries bring in the most profit, hens in deep litter next, and there's least profit of all from hens on free range, the way we keep them.'

He let that sink in, drinking his tea slowly. Then he said, weighing every word, 'Cost you a lot of money to put up a deep-litter house.' I agreed. 'But we could put battery cages in the stables,' I went on, 'or even in the garage.'

'No need to do that,' he said with great deliberation. 'If you start keeping 'ens in batteries, you won't 'ave my wages to pay.'

I knew he was deeply moved: it is only on such rare occasions that he forgets his aitches. It seemed that we would have to go on as we were. I supposed we could do some culling. He agreed that ''twouldn't be no use feeding birds as didn't lay'.

When we took the hens their midday mash I peered intently at them as they fought for the food. They could not have looked healthier, rushing after the old man as he moved from trough to trough. Then I noticed one stumbling and tripping over its wing. 'Look!' I yelled, diving into my pockets for the leaflets, where I had read

something about drooping wings. Sam put the bucket down, watched for a moment, then said accusingly, ''Tis an injury'.

'It's fowl paralysis,' I countered, having found the place. 'You must kill it, Sam.'

He snorted. 'Looks like an injury to me,' he muttered obstinately. 'Bird looks healthy enough.' The pullet squatted suddenly at his feet. 'She lays, you see,' he said in quiet triumph as he picked it up. I felt the wing carefully. It was not broken; neither, as far as my limited veterinary knowledge could tell, was it dislocated. Sam stuck his jaw out. 'I think 'tis some kind of injury,' he persisted; 'I don't like killing young things.' So we agreed to isolate the pullet.

The next day it laid, and his delight was touching. 'Ah,' he said, 'doesn't do to be in too much of a hurry. Once 'tis dead, 'tis dead, and you can't do nothing about it.' When it laid again the following day, Sam was jubilant; there couldn't be much wrong with it, he thought. On the third day it laid two soft eggs. That was nothing, Sam assured me, but he did not look quite so confident, even though he thought it was carrying its wing a little higher. On the fourth day, to my surprise, I found it perching; but when it flew down to feed it fell over on to its back and, though apparently quite happy in this position, was totally unable to get up. When I reported this to Sam I felt he did not believe me. It was funny, he thought, that it couldn't stand upright if it could fly on to a perch which was all of two feet off the ground.

The next day the pullet was upside-down again, 'Look, Sam,' I insisted, 'I can't keep coming out here to turn it the right way up. You'll have to kill it.'

He looked at me queerly. 'I 'aven't seen it upside-down,' he said with emphasis. I noticed the missing aitch, but I stuck to my guns. 'You must kill it,' I repeated, and went indoors.

Half way through breakfast I heard Sam's voice at the window: 'Are you quite sure you want that pullet killed?' I banged down my cup. 'Haven't you killed it yet?' I bellowed. He looked a little sly, a little triumphant. No, not yet, he hadn't. Why? Had it laid again? No, it hadn't actually laid, he explained, but it soon would: it had squatted at his feet, and what was more, he was pretty sure this time its wing was higher up. I disagreed. It was obviously paralysed. If we kept it much longer it would lose condition and no longer be fit for the table. Well, that of course was a different matter. If he had known I wanted something to eat, he would have killed it at once, though the Lord knew we weren't getting all that many eggs we could afford to eat our young pullets. He went off muttering, plainly disgusted with me. I returned to my cooling coffee with a sigh of relief, but not for long. Sam reappeared with the bird tucked under his arm, and I had to admit that it looked in the best of health.

'I just want you to feel its wing,' he said ingratiatingly. 'Just to be sure. 'Tisn't as if 'twas off its feed. 'Twould be a pity if we found out 'twas an injury after all. There now, just there: isn't that joint bigger than what the other one is, like as if it might be dislocated?'

It was exactly the same size, but I was beaten: he just could not bring himself to kill it. 'All right,' I said, 'put it back.'

I spent the next three days visiting the pullet and turning it the right way up. It seemed happy enough, but it did not lay the promised egg. On the ninth day of its incarceration I had to go to town. When I got back and asked after it Sam looked depressed. 'Hasn't laid yet,' he admitted. 'Right way up all day?' I quizzed. He shook his head sadly, like a man defeated. 'I can't understand it,' he said. 'It lay on its back, and when I picked it up it fell on its side, and yet 'twas up on the perch in the morning.' I waited. 'Tell you what,' he said, "tisn't no use keeping it. I'll kill it in the morning. Make a nice little dinner for you.'

(Spring 1963)

UNCOMMON ASSAULT

R. J. Jennings

Travelling through North Wales last year, I stopped the car to stretch my legs and eat a sandwich at Pont Petryal, a narrow bridge on the road from Ruthin to Cerrig-y-Druidion. To my right a narrow lane led through plantations of larch and spruce, past the source of the river Clwyd, up on to the Denbigh moors. On the left a fading sign pointed to Melin-y-Wig. Now I knew where we were. 'There is a gamekeeper's cottage and a lake around this bend in the road,' I said to my wife. 'I worked here before the war. I wonder what it looks like now.' We opened the gate and followed the path.

The track to the lake was overgrown, and we stepped through tall bracken down to the water's edge. I glanced into the reeds: yes, there it was, an old oak stake firmly embedded in the mud, with a short length of chain and a piece of wire netting, rusting with age, stapled to the wood –

the swan's enclosure. I gazed into the water momentarily and remembered; it was twenty-five years ago.

The midsummer day had been sweltering. From eight in the morning until five I had been working in the heather. The gnats had eaten their fill of me, and the back of my neck was red with sweat and sunburn. What I needed was a swim, but where?

Brought up in the Thames valley, I had learned to swim in the Cherwell and the Evenlode. Here in Denbighshire, where I had been sent on a reafforestation scheme, the difficulty was to find a place deep enough to bathe. In the mountain streams you could sometimes immerse yourself up to the waist, if you sat down, but that was a tame business compared to a dive from a river bank and a race across to the opposite side. I happened to mention this to my friend the keeper as we ate our lunch by a butt on the grouse moor. 'Well,' he said, 'if you want a swim, have one in the lake by my house. Let me know when you are coming, and I will shut up the swan.' That sounded good enough for me, and we arranged that I would call at half past six that evening.

I had seen the swan, a vicious ill-tempered aggressive creature, whose mate had died some years before. Every spring a natural urge compelled him to build a nest at one end of the lake. Then, as was to be expected, this solitary frustrated bird would be in his worst mood. Approach the water's edge, and he would hiss and make much fuss. Give him an opportunity and, like a farmyard gander, he would nip the calf of your leg. Chase him away, and he would finally retreat into the centre of the lake and show his anger by patrolling up and down, his beautiful neck pressed back into his wings, the wake from his powerful swimming turning up waves that rippled into the bank. But this show of temper had never impressed me; I was used to swans on the Thames. I had heard tales of men having a leg broken by a blow from a swan's wings, but I had never believed them. To me a swan was no more to be feared than a goose – inclined to be a bully perhaps, but harmless.

That evening I cycled the two miles from the farm where I lived to Petryal and made my way straight to the water. I saw no sign of the keeper and, not wishing to hinder him or interrupt his tea, I thought I would enjoy my swim without further ceremony. Glancing towards the far end of the lake, I caught a glimpse of the swan up-ending himself in the water; he was pulling weed from the muddy bottom and, as far as I was concerned, had not seen me.

Slipping into my bathing trunks behind some rhododendrons, I stepped on to a raft, took a deep breath and plunged into the cool water. A few strokes under the surface and I made for the far end of the lake. Then, suddenly, I received a violent blow on the back of my neck, another on the shoulder and, as I opened my eyes, something hit me on the forehead that nearly knocked me unconscious. I felt stunned for a moment or two but came to my senses when I felt my feet becoming entangled in weeds on the bottom of the lake. I kicked for the surface, gasping for breath. My shoulder felt paralysed and I began to realise that, unless I could regain the bank and stop swallowing water, I was in danger of being drowned. I retched and coughed, as I felt the cold spring water that fed the lake already in my lungs; but as I struck out weakly for the raft, a great white feathered body with beating threshing wings again pushed me under, so that I desperately choked for breath.

Now I knew what I was up against – the swan. On dry land I would have mastered him, but in his element I was coming off a

(A. F. Wiles)

bad second best. Again I struck out for the bank and again he attacked, this time savagely with open bill. I got a glimpse of his furious eye and saw his yellow-and-black face as he reached at me and beat me once more with his wings. He rose from the water and I felt his great feet on my neck; again his wings rained blows on my head. Half stunned and weakening I was wondering how much longer I could last, when I felt my feet on something solid. I struck out again, stumbled and fell forward in a mass of weed and mud at the edge of the lake. I stood up and staggered on to dry land.

Bruised and panting I watched the swan retreat, no worse for the encounter. For a couple of minutes he swam furiously up and down the lake; then he made for the far end to preen his feathers, leaving me to nurse my wounds and wash off the mud. I dressed and, feeling the worse for wear, discreetly mounted my bicycle. As I passed the end of the lake near the road, the swan up-ended himself several times in the water.

I saw the keeper the following afternoon and thought I discerned a twinkle in his eye as he said, 'Hullo! What have you been doing to your face? You've scratched it on something; and there's a nasty mark on your nose. Have you had a fight?' Then, before I could reply, 'By the way, I had to go out yesterday tea-time. Don't forget now, let me know when you're coming for that swim. I'll shut the swan up.' Had he watched from the wood? I still wonder.

(Winter 1963)

THE PONY PROBLEM

Patrick Dobbs

Hiking over the mountains may be fine for holiday-makers, but it is no good at all for working farmers like myself. I am a good walker and still a year or two under thirty, but I decided very early in my sheep-farming career that a pony, though not essential, came before such luxuries as an oven, a wife and a doormat. Advice from kind neighbours, especially those with animals to sell, was given freely.

The main point seemed to be to get something small, sure-footed, reliable, hardy, quiet and strong. I must forget about astonishing the natives on a high-class hunter or enjoying the delights of a dainty hack; nor must I fall for the showy carriage or glossy coat of an arab or a mincing thoroughbred. It was a working-man's horse I needed – one that would pull tree stumps all the morning, move the cows in the afternoon and allow the dogs to run round her legs while collecting the sheep after tea.

I found my cob at the Llanybyther sales. She was sound and solid, a black mare by Llwynog y Garth. There was no difficulty about breaking her in; she scarcely arched her back when I saddled her for the first time and was never hot-headed or awkward in the noisiest traffic. She is easy to catch, works unshod without going lame, carries the dog when he is tired, herds cattle like a cow-pony and stands untied to a trailing rein on the open mountain. She is called Polly, which describes her rather well: steady and worthy and all that, yet somehow not exciting.

I am not running down the virtues of hardiness, reliability, strength and all the rest of it; but there is no getting away from the fact that the real mountainy men, the big sheep farmers like the Watkins of Trecastle, the pony fanciers like Idris Hope of Stangau and the man with the sheepwalk next to mine, Gwynfor Evans of Panty-gwin, all ride something with a bit of class about it – thoroughbred on one side of the face at least, as they say. Beside their

mounts my Polly looks, though I hate to admit it, like something out of a cart.

Until this summer I resigned myself to this rather common form of transport. Pride of ownership, or keeping up with the Joneses if you like, would have to wait. I am at the bottom of the farming ladder; the frills must not come until the foundations are unshakeable. But I have had a visit from a friend – a friend with a horse. This animal is everything Polly is not – fast, showy, graceful; a nervy excitable ride and inclined to shy at traffic, rocks and tree stumps, but what a delight, the flashing eyes and quivering muscles eager to go! How clumsy is the cob after that blue-blooded aristocrat!

Now I am unsettled. It is not until you have lived with solid worth for a year or two that you realise what you really want is beauty and speed; that is why so many people get divorces. I go to the horse sales at Hereford and plan a trip to Dublin in August. I scan advertisement columns and talk to friends. The main difficulty, of course, is financial; I cannnot expect what I want under three figures and then some – young and sound, without a blemish and fit for a king to ride at a wedding.

I have also become attached to Polly in a quiet unemotional way; I would not like to part with her. Perhaps I will let her raise a family; she is a good roomy mare and would throw a fine colt to a thoroughbred horse. But then I would not get any money to buy the next one. Perhaps I could hire her out to the pony trekkers, only they sometimes knock their mounts about a bit. Perhaps, after all, I will be riding her over the mountain for another twelvemonth, and get my dream horse the same time as I have my holiday – next year, always next year.

(Winter 1963)

Connor Pass, Co. Kerry. (J. E. Jenkins)

TOUGH TIMES

GRANNY, GET YOUR GUN

Ruth Wilson

Life wasn't easy for my grandmother, Agnes Perret. Being left a widow with an eight-year-old child brought difficulties enough. To run a farm single-handed in an age when, to most people, 'women's emancipation' meant something vaguely connected with female black slaves, was nearly impossible. But, to Gran, all things were possible given the will, the determination and the courage. Gran had all three – and finally they were her downfall.

It was 1907. After her husband's premature death, Gran determined to keep the farm in Herefordshire near the Welsh border as a future legacy for young Edith. She managed to hire two labourers from the nearby village who came in daily. More by luck than judgement, the major pitfalls of that first year were avoided. Christmas found the family quietly rejoicing. The stock thrived. The harvest had been good and all the fattened birds were, even now, being demolished on other families' festive tables. Gran knew that there was hard work ahead, but who was afraid of hard work? It was a time for optimism.

Boxing Day came cold but clear. The men had been given a holiday, but there were cows to be milked and stock to be fed. As Gran and little Edith tackled the chores together, they soon became aware of the clamour of the hunt. Gran listened uneasily to the distant baying. She had been born and brought up in Herefordshire, but a pack of hounds and a dozen excited men on sweating horses, chasing a solitary fox did little, in her estimation, towards keeping down the fox population – especially as she strongly suspected that they were rearing cubs. Foxes skulking around Grandmother's poultry were rewarded with a double blast from a shot-gun.

This attitude did not make her very popular with the hunt. She was even less popular when she forbade them to ride over her land. A small farm could ill afford broken fences and trampled crops. But, first and foremost, Gran considered fox-hunting cruel, indulged in for the pleasure of the huntsmen rather than the extermination of the fox.

The clamouring grew louder and the suspicion that they were on her land hardened into certainty. 'Mother, look!' cried Edith, pointing up at the hillside. A small brown shadow was flowing down the field. A ray of wintry sun touched it and the brown became flame. Then it melted into the shadow of the hedge and was hidden from view. Anxiously Gran scanned the wooded hilltop. As the leader of the pack of hounds came into view, so again did the fox. It rounded the byre and headed across the yard. With bulging eyes and lolling tongue it came loping, saliva coating its muzzle and chest. Ribs heaving and fine brush dragging the ground, it passed within a yard of Gran's skirts and through the open door of the barn.

Completely disconcerted, Gran stood for a moment, then she leaped into action. 'Edith. Run and get the gun – quickly. And bring some bird-shot.' Even as she spoke, Gran was closing the heavy barn door and sliding in the bolt. The child flew across the yard and into the house.

The hounds were in victorious tongue as they poured down the long field. Their leader plunged through the hedge and raced the returning child across the yard to fling itself against the barn door.

Gran snatched the shot-gun from the girl and ordered her into the house. The pack was streaming into the yard as she loaded a cartridge into each barrel. Hounds were everywhere – leaping, snapping, yelping with frustrated fury. They scratched and bit at the wood that separated them from their prey and skirmished savagely with each other. Gran stood to one side, ashen-faced, the shot-gun held tightly across her chest. Young Edith stood in the kitchen doorway, eyes bright with fearful excitement.

Horsemen were tally-hoing down the hill and the first red coat jumped the hedge. Then the yard was full of riders; the musty smell of horse-sweat almost overpowering.

The Master gestured furiously with his crop. 'Get that door open!' he bellowed. An eager young member began to dismount.

'Stay where you are,' Gran shouted above the clamour of demented hounds. Taken unaware, the man hesitated. A dozen pairs of astonished eyes turned upon the woman standing quietly in the turmoil of the yard. Slowly the gun muzzle swung down and levelled at the huntsmen. 'Now, whip up your hounds and get off my land.'

There was a moment of stunned incredulity. It was inconceivable that anyone should give sanctuary to a fox. Was it possible that this insignificant woman in her drab working clothes could defy the members of the hunt? Of course not. The Master turned a contemptuous back. He gestured to the eager young member. 'Open that door.'

With the gun rock-steady in her hands. Gran shouted 'Get off my land or I'll fire.' The young man hesitated and looked at the Master for a lead. The Master's face turned scarlet with fury and affront. 'Stand back, woman, if you know what's good for you. Put up that gun this instant.' Slowly Gran took off the safety catch.

'For the last time of telling – leave my land or I'll fire,' came her answer. Both faces were equally grim, equally determined. Staring into the woman's unwavering eyes, the Master hesitated. Then his horse pranced skittishly and the spell was broken. Outraged authority returned in full.

'What are you waiting for, man? Open

'Bird-shot whined over the Master's head . . .' (Brian Walker)

that door,' he ordered. As the bolt was being withdrawn, Gran elevated the gun barrel and tightened her finger on the trigger.

The explosion scattered the hounds and set the startled horses whirling. Bird-shot whined over the Master's head. The fringe pellets, already fanning out, peppered the rump of his mount. Up reared the horse, forelegs shredding the air. With a whinny of terror it bolted blindly down the lane. The Master, stirrups lost, clung desperately around its neck. A dozen pairs of startled eyes watched his white-breeched buttocks recede, wildly bobbing, into the distance.

Gran's voice rose above the pandemonium. 'Now, whip up those hounds and get off my land.' The members took one look into the black mouth of the undischarged barrel aimed into their midst. Within minutes the yard was empty, save for one lone figure leaning weakly against the wall.

That afternoon, as dusk fell, Gran cautiously opened the barn door and held it ajar. From out of the darkness stepped the fox. Unafraid, it passed beneath her outstretched arm. Trotting daintily, it negotiated the churned-up yard with its odours of hound, horse and man, and disappeared up the hill. Later that evening Gran wrote a letter of apology and addressed it to the Master's horse.

They never forgave her. Within weeks her labourers had been offered jobs at a rate of pay she could not match. No one would work for her. She could not blame them. They could not afford to take sides. Her stock fetched the lowest prices at market. No casual labour could be hired for planting and harvesting. Her fruit went unsold and rotted on the trees.

Within two years, mother and daughter watched the farm and all it contained come under the auctioneer's hammer. The sale was well attended but the bidding was

exceedingly low. With head held high and back ramrod-straight, Gran took her daughter by the hand and they shook the soil of the country from their feet.

Years later, listening to this favourite story for the umpteenth time, I asked my grandmother if she ever regretted her stand. 'Never,' she said. 'If you bend a principle for personal convenience, then it is not a principle. However,' she added ruefully, 'I sometimes wish I had aimed lower!'

(Spring 1982)

POTATO PICKERS

Like feeding rooks, the dark-gowned
  women pick
Ploughed-up potatoes from November
  mud.
The wind draws chill. On neighbouring
  roof and rick
The white flower, frost, lies in half-
  opened bud.
Unblessed by sunlight goes the
  cowering band.
Down the long furrows tread the
  patient feet,
Cumbered with clay from this too heavy
  land,
Robbed by the seeping damp of
  comfort's heat.
Shrill-voiced, the labourers gather in a
  flock.
Their loud talk rasps the sky, filing from
  day
Its golden quiet. Struck from their
  nature's rock,
A rill of laughter floods the miry way;
And fortitude behind each eye's keen
  stare
Defies the louring of the autumn air.
G. J. Blundell (Autumn 1964)

A MEMORY OF ELMS

Felled into the sick length
of their own shadows,
they lay
coffined in grass,
creeping moss and lichen
for shrouds.
No cross in this graveyard,
no stone for remembering.
Only the wind, sweeping
across unsheltered fields,
laments,
recalls the embrace
of their rough branches;
and displaced rooks,
lost
in a strange landscape,
wear black for funerals.

Lois Clark (Autumn 1977)

(D. Macer Wright)

(Stuart Seager)

(Kenneth Scowen)

THE BLOCKLEY RIOTS:
AN EYE-WITNESS ACCOUNT

H. E. McL. Icely

'A double depression hit the North Cotswold village of Blockley in the 1870s. 'The men worked on farms or in industries dependent on farming, which experienced a disastrous decline. The women and girls were employed in silk-throwing mills which, in a free-trade system, were unable to compete with the French silk industry, recovering rapidly after the Franco-Prussian war. By 1878 the poor of the village were near starvation, and there happened to be in the neighbourhood at that time a watchful keeper who made poaching unusually difficult. To add to its troubles the village was experiencing its last serious smallpox epidemic.

This was no time to harry those guilty of minor misdemeanours; but Sergeant Drury, who later proved himself to be a humane and considerate policeman, made the mistake of seeing too much. He was on the track of all the poachers reported to him, with results that are recorded in the manuscript journal of R. B. Belcher, a fine Liberal Nonconformist resident of the period. He wrote: 'Two innocent young men fled from the village and never returned, because they had picked up a rabbit which they found in a snare. Another was arrested for picking up three partridge eggs which had been placed on the bare ground by the keeper. Yet another who was charged with poaching was put to the expense of £8 for a lawyer and a cartload of witnesses to establish his innocence . . . Oliver B. was stopped on his way home by a bough blown off a tree, which had obstructed the traffic for many days. He took the bough into his trap and openly put it into his garden. Our zealous policeman obtained a warrant and B. was locked up in the police cell two days and night, and committed to Worcester Sessions, where he was acquitted'.

With all this and much more to his discredit in the possibly not very clear minds of his neighbours, Sergeant Drury chose to pay a routine visit to the Crown Inn one Saturday night at closing time. The events that followed were described to Miss Mary Dee, whose mother's people, the Westmacotts, built and owned the big mill in the village, by a woman who died there in 1942 at the age of seventy-three.

'It were sixty yur agoo come the twenty-sixth o' March,' said the old lady, 'an I were nine. I can see that crowd now, comin' along by 'Erbert's the butcher's, an' it were 'Erberts at the Crown too. It all come about over a policeman we 'ad 'ere. Everybody 'ated 'im. 'E were one o' them slick sneakin' sort o' men. If you kicked a stun along the street, 'e were arter you an' threatenin' what 'e'd do to you. Well, that day 'e 'ad took about a dozen Blockley men to Shipston, an' I suppose thur was fine goin's on over thur arter the trial. Anyway Major Bird from Barton as was the magistrate that day, 'e warned the old bobby not to goo up into Blockley that night; but 'e were that brazen, o' course, 'e went.

'Mrs Pate Keyte in Lower Street were servant at the Crown at the time an' 'er see it all; a-wevver 'er see the start of it. On the Sat'day night it were, at ten o'clock 'e must needs goo up into the Crown an' peep over the settle. Thur they was a-sitten' an' a-drinkin', many of 'em 'alf drunk an' when they see'd 'is 'ead come over the top o' the settle, somebody banged a quart pot o' beer at it an' 'it it. Well, as I says, 'e showed 'is 'ead over the settle. That done it. 'E didn't ought to 'a done that, an' as soon as 'e could see arter the beer 'it 'im, 'e took to 'is 'eels an' they arter 'im along i' the 'Igh Street.

'When the runnin' started every door along the street opened an' out come somebody else to join in. 'E made off straight down the churchyard to 'is 'ome, they followin'. The police station in them days was only one o' them 'ouses as is the police station today. The blacksmith lived in t'other 'ouse. Well, I were the oldest in our 'ouse among the children, an' I were still up. My mother were a-darnin' stockin's an' when 'er 'eeard the runnin' down went the stockin's an' off 'er went an' o' course I 'ad to follow 'er. It took most o' the night an' my mother said 'er'd larrup me, but 'er never did.

'Well, 'e took off down the churchyard, an' I nipped down be'ind 'em as near as I deeard an' got up on the mill wall an' dangled me legs over the top, an' o' course I could see all as went on. Well, 'e got to 'is 'ouse an' got inside. By this time they was a 'owlin' mob, an' they was determined to get 'im. They smashed the gate, pulled the gateposts down, battered the door down an' got 'im. 'E an' 'is wife was stood together at the top o' the stairs. Them as couldn't get in throwed stuns at the winders an' broke every winder in both

THE STONE-BREAKER

B. Crocker

Half a century ago the outlook was grim for the old, disabled and impecunious countryman. If totally unfit, he had nothing to look forward to but the workhouse and the pauper's uniform of drabette coat, check neckcloth and fustian trousers; but as long as he could move arms and shoulders the guardians considered him capable of breaking down block stone to road-metal size, thus saving the ratepayers at least three shillings a week. Stone breaking required skill but was nevertheless regarded as the lowest form of labour, and no able-bodied man would undertake it except of necessity. Those old-timers worked under almost impossible conditions. On Sourton Down, Devon, a blind man with bruised and bleeding fingers used to break stone into the proper grades by touch. His little girl, carrying his tools, led him to his heap before she went to school and collected him at the end of the day. A man who, through neglected rheumatism, had to go to work on crutches carried his hammers in a sack slung over his shoulder. The sack acted as a cloak when it rained; there was no other shelter. A carter, both of whose legs had been broken through an accident at work, was put on to stone-breaking as soon as he could hobble with the aid of two sticks. His wife carried his tools, then went back to do the heavy work for the farmer's wife. As a road inspector I came on many such cases, so I am not one of those who sigh for the good old days. *(Autumn 1959)* 'ouses. The old 'ooman the blacksmith's wife were frit pretty near to death. Somebody fetched the bobby's wife out an' shut 'er up; 'er couldn't stop thur – look at all they stuns a-flyin'.

'Well, they fetched 'im out an' they mauled 'im an' they pummelled 'im an' then they dipped 'im in that brook. It weren't railed in in them days, an' they ducked 'im in thur a time or two, an' Pate Keyte as lives in Lower Street, 'is father an' Oliver Eastbury carried 'im into Pate Keyte's 'ouse an' locked the door. Oliver Eastbury as 'ad 'elped to knock 'im about, 'e carried 'im in, carried 'im upstairs, washed 'im – an' 'e wanted washin' – an' stayed by 'im all night. You know they'd a' killed 'im if somebody 'adn't fetched 'im away from 'em, for by that time they 'ad very near killed 'im.

'Thur were another bobby down at Draycott at that time, an' 'e 'appened to be in Blockley that night; but when 'e showed up they threatened 'e that if 'e didn't clear off, they'd serve 'e the same. At first 'e didn't seem to want to goo, so some on 'em took an' pitched 'e over the wall an' then 'e took off; but 'e got the sack for it.

'That settled the two bobbies, but just arter the clock finished strikin' twelve they took an' fetched 'em out o' their beds. Five got away, but five was took. They was 'Arry Clarke, Rube Carter, George Matthews, Oliver Eastbury an' 'Arry Smith. Jim Webb was one as got away, an' 'e were a ring-leader. Four on 'em got eighteen months, an' 'Arry Smith – Turner Smith they called 'im on account of 'is work – 'e got twelve months, but 'e were innocent. The worst on 'em got away, an' for years an' years thur were a warrant out agin 'em.

'When all them men 'ad done their time at 'Ooster thur were great doin's the day they come 'ome. They closed the mill – that were Smith's mill – an' all the women wi' tin cans an' kettles an' pots an' pans an' trays went down to the station to meet 'em an' drummed 'em up into the village.'

(Winter 1961)

MINER'S WIFE

Winifred Foley

Granny was left a widow at nineteen when her young husband Enoch, a miner in the Forest of Dean, died of pneumonia. The previous week he had been gathering acorns in pouring rain to store for the pig he had just brought. She let the tiny cottage for eighteen pence a week, took her baby Charlie home to her parents and went back to service to earn her keep and his. Three years later she married again. Bob too was a miner, dour, handsome and inarticulate. His vocabulary consisted mostly of grunts, but Granny's ebullience balanced the scales. In her little cottage, next to one owned by Enoch's sister, they produced and brought up seven girls and a boy.

Olive, the eldest, was staid and reliable, went off to service at thirteen, stuck her jobs well and married a steady miner, then broke the conformity by emigrating with him to America. Beattie came next, a nymphomaniacal beauty, wily-tongued, shallow and deviously clever for her own ends. Gladys was, if possible, dourer than her father, plain, self-righteous and lacking in humour; she 'got religion' at an early age. Slow, good-tempered Win was thought to be 'a bit short of her buttons', but eventually went into service and rose to the position of cook. Lois – christened Lous, for Grancher could not spell – was attractive, intelligent and charming and enhanced the status of the family by marrying a policeman. Phyl was the family clown, droll and endearing, known to bring half a smile even to Grancher's face; he never managed to lift the two corners of his mouth at the same time. The youngest girl was Elsie, more beautiful than Beattie and utterly different in character. She was innately immaculate in her person and managed to look neat and tidy in whatever Granny could forage to cover her. Last came Stan, a delicate little boy, spoilt by his doting sisters.

Though Granny often shook her head at the bewildering diversity of her offspring, she tried to favour none especially. "Tain't right to make poop o' one an' pudden o' another' was her philosophy. But she adored Elsie and was never quite the same, the neighbours said, after her early death from consumption.

It was impossible to make do for this large family with the few shillings Grancher brought home from the pit. He had, of course, the miner's right to a fuel allowance of twelve hundredweight a month, so coal was no problem. Clothes never came out of a shop; daughters in service sent parcels home. Paper had often to be stuck into boots to keep bare soles off the ground. But food was the major worry. 'It's like this, Mr Westaway,' Granny told the grocer frankly. 'I don't see no 'opes o' keepin' out o' your debt an' me keepin' my

young 'uns out o' the graveyard from famishment. But if you'll let us 'ave the victuals an' pay what I can, if the Lard do spare us, when they be growned up an' off me 'ands, you shall be paid every penny.'

Mr Westaway never failed to deliver the primitive necessities, and in time Granny paid up, true to her word. I was about six years old by then, my father – her first child Charlie – having married and gone to live next door with my great-aunt. Granny could not read nor write nor reckon herself. She cried with relief when old Westaway told her she was out of debt and gave her a seedy cake for commission. Then she lifted her skirts and did a little dance in the yard to celebrate the honourable end of her bankruptcy.

She regarded the Almighty as the provider of any bit of luck that came her way, and blamed the devil for the rest. Once. during a long drought, when the village well had dried to a trickle, she was anxious to 'dab out a bit o' weshin''. 'Bob,' she said, 'thee'll 'ave to 'elp I vetch a bathful from the Splashes.' This meant a mile walk down a steeply wooded hillside to a stream in the forest. Precious quantities of the water were lost as they struggled back, each holding a handle of the big zinc bath. Sweating and puffing, they had just got to the cottage door when the handle came off Granny's end and all the water was wasted over the yard. She took a full minute to get her breath; then, with a withering look skywards, she announced, 'If cleanliness be next to godliness, 'twas a pity 'Im didn't see fit to send down a drap more rain.' During the night an almighty thunderstorm rumbled across the sky, forked lightning kept our heads under the patchwork quilts, and the torrential rain found its way through every leaky roof in the village. 'I shall 'a' to be a bit more polite 'ow I do ask for things in the future,' said Granny. She was by no means house-proud and would always find time to 'quat on 'er 'arse' for a gossip: 'Work 'll kip, an' a bit o' good scandal 'as more flavour when 'tis 'ot.' One day when she was having a long natter over the gate with a passer-by, I decided to clean up for her. Granny's method was to pick up the rag mat for a shake in the yard, to shovel the ashes from under the huge grate into a bucket, to rub the steel fender and fire-irons with a bit of damp rag dipped in the finer ashes, then to sweep the floor, replace the mat and rub a duster over the few sticks of furniture. I decided to sweep the ashes with the hard broom straight out into the yard over the mat. When I had finished the place looked like the aftermath of a volcanic eruption. My eyes were smarting, the mat was smouldering under the hot ash, and dust was settling in choking layers on everything.

'I be cleaning up for you, Granny,' I announced. Mam would have given me a good clout on the ear, but Granny was pleased; I could see it by the laughter twitching the corners of her mouth. 'Bless my soul, so you be. There's a reglar little 'oman 'er is, cleanin' up for 'er old Granny. 'Ere,' and she took a halfpenny from the tin on the mantelpiece where she kept her housekeeping money, 'you goo off to the shop an' buy some sweeties for bein' a good little wench.'

(Winter 1969)

TAIL CORN

Derbyshire farm worker's description of tall and very thin Wesleyan minister: ''E looked as if 'e lived on buttervlies an' 'ad to ketch 'em vurst.' *(Spring 1957)*

Buckinghamshire woman, whose son Harry was difficult to get up in the morning, said to him: 'If you don't get up I'll knock you down.' *(Spring 1977)*

Somerset gardener: ''Er be a good potato, 'er be. Do 'ee see 'er lovely blue eyes?'
(Spring 1952)

Two Herefordshire farmers, each separately describing a very thin man: ''E's as thin as a snipe's gut' and ''E's so thin, that if th' door opened an' nobody come through – that 'ud be 'im!' *(Autumn 1975)*

Somerset villager to church-goer: ''Ave vicar started readin' Genesis yet? 'E 'ave? Then I mun get my beans in this week.' *(Spring 1972)*

The village pond at Wroxton, Oxfordshire. (Kenneth A. Coldman)

AT PLAY

MEMORIES OF DROMAGH FAIR

Andrew Forrest

It is well nigh impossible now for anyone to visualise what Dromagh Fair was like: one big day in the year for the people of south-west Munster, sixty years ago. The world and his wife, and his sons and daughters too, went to Dromagh Fair; and they went year after year. They went to sell and buy, to fight and have fun. And boy, did they have it! They went to the fair to drink and get drunk; and they sure did that too. As I write, I have before me a copy of the 'Schedule of the Tolls and Customs' which shows that every article one could possibly require was for sale, and

'Fine respectable farmers, grand heavy men, dressed to kill'. (Raymond Piper)

at the right price.

I was a mere lad when I attended the last couple of fairs; yet the passing of a lifetime has failed to dim the memory of them. Even then the sun was setting for Dromagh. Its best days were over; the mines were closed, the miners gone. The pits in Dysart, Lisnacon, Coolclough and the Island were flooded, and all I remember of Dysart coal was one big pit pump that held up the gable-end of old Hannah Smallman's cabin.

At the fair it was splendid to see all the fine respectable farmers, grand heavy men, dressed to kill, with big stiff collars and bowler hats. Only in London today will you find such an array of bowlers. I remember those farmers of long ago, every one of them weighing twenty stone or more, with big bellies out in them, fine easy-going men, their watch-chains suspended from side to side. There was no 'fright' in them, and every one brought two or three men and a gossoon to mind pigs and cattle, turn and turn about. Far above the gossoon, but as far below the farm worker, was the servant boy; at the fair the worker ordered him about, and he in turn kicked around the gossoon. But the gossoon usually ended up in complete charge, as the boss and his men were soon blotto, with porter at four-pence a gallon.

There is no mention of the stick man in the schedule, but to my mind he was important. Several stick sellers attended the fair, each with a big bundle of ash plants, cut to measure and retailing at 2d. each. Every servant boy spent a good part of the day buying, testing and breaking sticks, like officers testing swords before battle. The test was always carried out after purchase, and every poor-quality ash plant was discarded – broken. If the stick men did not clear their stocks at the fair, they sold the rest as job lots to schoolmasters. In that way the stick men contributed to higher education, for the rejects were broken across the bare legs of pupils in the summer. The fair was held in May.

According to the schedule, hawkers were charged 2d. for the right to peddle their wares at the fair; but beggars were admitted free. That was one reason, I suppose, why every beggar in Ireland worth his salt landed in Dromagh for the fair. Cork beggars, Kerry beggars, Limerick beggars, Dublin and foreign beggars, all made a point of hitting Dromagh; and they did well. It was considered the height of bad form to refuse to give alms. I remember several blind beggars and their dogs, and the curious thing about the dogs was that they had their eyes shut too, apparently having come to regard this as the thing to do. Gossoon though I was at the time, I recall the women beggars coming to me and saying, 'Kind gentleman, give me a penny to buy bread'. A trick of genius on someone's part, the 'Kind gentleman' was sure to work wonders on a lad of ten or eleven years, being in great contrast to the treatment I received from almost everyone else at the fair. They called me a 'cursid mope' or commanded me to 'mind that beast', as the case might be.

Once the farmer had disposed of his cattle, his men were free for the day; and it was always interesting to watch a 'dale' being made. One such transaction concerned a pig. The owner had brought it in a donkey car all the way from beyond Macroom, and he was anxious to sell.

'Would ye be selling d' oul' crampy now by any chance?' asked the buyer sarcastically.

'The loike o' him for a pig niver stood the fair, God bless him,' replied the man from beyond Macroom, at the same time giving the creature a clout on the ear.

'Huh-huh,' exclaimed the buyer, 'give him his country till we see is he crampy.'

Then the man from outside Macroom did a fool thing; he let the pig out of the crib. That was the signal for every servant boy at the fair to test his stick. No sooner had the pig hit the ground than he got a cut of an ash plant across the hams and, like a rocket, away with him down through the fair. Right and left he dodged, squealing like a demon, sending the pedlars' stands flying in all direction. No sooner would he emerge from under one stand than he would take a few more cuts; then off with him again amid cheers and curses and shouts of 'Stop that crampy pig'.

Finally the shout went up, 'Who owns the crampy?' Someone answered, 'A bucock of a farmer from Macroom, an' may the divel sweep the two of 'em.' Then developed the father and mother of a faction fight. All the men from Macroom side supported their man. They would catch the crampy, they said. Just as they would be closing in on him, some scut would give the pig another cut of a plant: then off, with a dozen or so Macroom men in hot pursuit. In the meantime the pig would have gone like the hammers of hell to some other part of the fair.

Then there was the fellow who sold old clothes, and another who dealt in discarded clothing. There was a difference between them, and I am sorry to recall that women from all over Munster could be seen picking and poking in the stall where discarded clothing was sold, like ants in a disturbed ant-heap. Meanwhile, up at the porter tents, the men were singing, drinking, back-slapping and placing orders for many gallons of the 'crater' with men from more remote areas. It is an understatement that as many as a hundred 'distillery owners' came every year to Dromagh.

I am not saying that people drank nothing but whisky and poteen, but they certainly took enough of both. And every animal on the farm got a good 'trogh' of poteen at regular intervals; they wanted no T.B. eradication scheme. The alleged crampy pig was two-and-a-half hundredweight and by no means finished to kill. And do you think for a minute that the donkey which hauled that pig from outside Macroom did not get his hot drop before starting on the twenty-five Irish miles trot? So did the pig for that matter.

There was an item on the schedule, 'Every Victualler's Boiling Pot'; and in those days there were many of these pots supplying boiled meat of every description, and some that defied description. Into them went pigs' heads, pigs' crubeens, whole porkers, whole cows and mutton; and the gourmet could order any meat he fancied, to be eaten then and there. A man whom I accompanied to the fair said on his way home that it was donkey meat they had given him, 'an' what's more, 'twas a bit of hind-quarter from under the breeching'.

Needless to say, Dromagh Fair had its quota of quacks: the black man pulling teeth, the men with the 'bottle for pains' and the 'bottle to prevent old age'. And talk about business! I can still remember the quack with a 'bottle for everything', shouting at the top of his voice: 'O people of Dromagh, O possessors of wealth, every-thing that is round is not a nut, nor is everything long a banana, nor is everything that is red meat, nor everything tawny a date. O people of Dromagh, this precious bottle, whose value no money can equal, with what sum will you open the bidding for it?' The 'bottle to cure everything' sold like hot cakes. It helped people to enjoy life – or to endure it.

(Autumn 1965)

A SADDLER'S BELLS

George Ewart Evans

Herbert Bayles was saddler and harness-maker in the Suffolk village of Stradbroke, where he was born in 1861 and died seventy-five years later. Of slight build, with sensitive features, he wore in later years a large drooping moustache which combined with the twinkle in his eye to give him an air of good-humoured benevolence. In addition to running his own business he was telegraph-messenger and, for forty-seven years of his working life, verger, steeple-keeper and clock-winder, as his father and grand-father had been before him.

Only rarely did his duties clash. Then his friend Harry Webb, the postmaster, was usually involved; telegrams, even when they were tapped out in Morse code on the one line that kept Stradbroke in touch with the world, would wait for no man. The postmaster summoned his messenger by stepping out of his side door and ringing a small handbell to a set formula: *a-ding-a-ding* seven times, with a peremptory coda *A-DING*. At the sound Herbert would drop the harness he was working on, throw his apron over the counter, grab his jacket and hurry to the post office to earn his fee – twopence or more according to distance. On one occasion the brisk *a-ding-a-ding* found him in the tower astride the bell-frame, greasing the bells ready for the Easter services. As he took some time to extricate himself, Harry kept popping in and out of his office, and the furious ringing of his little bell brought the mild comment from wondering neighbours: 'Harry's whoolly riled. Harbut 'on't come!'

Bell-ringing was as important to Herbert as his business. He specialised in the handbells and had a fine collection of fifty-six, the largest of which was an inscribed presentation E flat, as wide across the mouth as a small pail. At the other end of the scale was Herbert's own particular bell, the smallest in his collection. This was often filled with whisky on an outing.

One of the choir boys who was in the handbell team has described how Herbert

THE BATSMAN'S BETROTHED

She walks around the boundaries late
beneath the plane-trees by the gate
next the sight-screen betimes she waits
from habit or from sorrow

One summer in the grass she lay
while bowlers toiled and he made hay
what if my man be called away
she thought and feared tomorrow

He was she paled the season died
a letter came she cried she cried
widow am I before a bride
I've lost my dashing fellow

She walks around the boundaries late
beneath the plane-trees by the gate
where the hedgerow begins to plait
the briar with the willow
Jeff Cloves (Summer 1986)

prepared them for these ringers' outings at the Christmas season. He wrote the tunes out on paper which he pasted on large sheets of cardboard and stood on an easel. The young ringers grouped themselves in a half circle about him. It did not matter that none could read music; each bell was given a number, and these were written plainly in large figures with blue and red pencil. Then the sequences were practised until every boy knew precisely his entrances and exits in the various patterns of sound.

During the 1914–18 war most of the handbell ringers were, perforce, young boys; and the verger taught them, in addition to the more usual programme, contemporary 'pops' like 'Tipperary', 'Keep the Home-fires Burning' and 'Pack Up Your Troubles'. This kept them interested enough to come regularly to practices. Herbert often worked on these tunes in his shop when he should have been finishing a farmer's harness. He would experiment with one, humming it over to himself to get the note, and having identified it, immediately convert it into its appropriate figure. If the farmer came for his harness, Herbert hurriedly thrust the numbered sheet under the counter and picked up awl, needle and thread.

One of his most important jobs at the beginning of this century was to toll the death bell. The tenor was used for this, but first it had to be raised – no easy matter for a small man, since it weighed more than a ton. Herbert often got Fred Amies, the blacksmith's son, to help him. Once the bell was raised, mouth uppermost, and set against the bell-stay, the verger could manage by himself. He placed his watch on the window-sill and kept his eyes steadily on it. Exactly five minutes after raising he pulled the rope just the required amount, and the bell, being set at handstroke, went through its revolution and came to rest at backstroke, giving one blow of the clapper against the metal. This manoeuvre called for fine judgement and the skill of an experienced ringer; it would have been easy to muff it altogether.

Herbert rang the bell once every five minutes for an hour, following the ritual with utmost care, both to preserve his reputation as a ringer and to ensure that the dead man got full measure of scrupulously observed respect. In the intervals he would record at the side of the ringing-chamber window the date and the age of the deceased. There were scores of entries in black pencil on the limewash; and also one or two special records of tolling with clappers muffled on the deaths of Queen Victoria and Edward VII. Alongside this rather sombre list was a sketch in blue and red pencil of a memorable sunset that had touched the old verger's imagination as he stood at the west window waiting for the minutes to go by. Unfortunately a tidy-minded restorer has since cleaned up the bell-chamber, and this record of part of Herbert's life has proved as evanescent as the sound of his bells.

(Winter 1963)

A CORNISH BAY

Diana Hopkinson

It is fifty years since, as a child of five, I spent the first of many summers with my brother and sister at Trethias Farm, three miles from Padstow. Nearly every day we went over the fields and down the lane, through a shady tunnel of arching tamarisk trees, to Treyarnon Bay. Just before the gate, where the low cliffs opened out, I could hear the beat of the waves. I hurried towards the sound, my heart echoing their beat in excitement. If the day was calm and the tide low, I knew from the gentle whisper that there would be only a faint lapping of the waves, like glinting opals, brushing the wide sands, still wet from the receding tide. My toes curled in my dust-laden sandals as I thought of my feet soon to tread the firm cool ribbing of the sand. Sometimes I heard a rough sea at high tide crashing quite near, and feared to meet a terrible army of waves sweeping up the road to engulf me.

This pattern of joy and fear at the approach to the bay was repeated among the small coves and dunes which bordered it. On the sand-hills I had seen the bleached skull of a horse crowned with a circlet of barbed wire, marram grass growing through its nostrils, for this was the grave-yard of the horses from the farm. Beyond these scattered bones, where the silver powdered sand met the crisp turf, I found the essence of blue and pink – the truth of these colours mingling where the sea holly sharpened its claws against the flowering trumpets of convolvulus. Shells like rose petals hid among the rough mussels; and the blue butterflies settled on the flowers of rest-harrow. Azures, cobalts and tur-quoises set against the roses, the rubies and the crimsons.

Some coves held treasure in cowrie shells or broken glass washed by the tides into jewels, for which my fingers combed the coarse sands. Others trapped wrecks after storm: oranges, a lifebelt of cork or the green lobes of fishing-floats covered in nets, to hang later from the rafters of the kitchen.

Why were those Negroes sitting astride that upturned boat as it drifted into the bay, and singing 'It's a Long Way to Tipperary' early in the morning? The farmer collecting seaweed with his horse and cart waded out to haul them in. They were no Negroes, for the year was 1917 and the submarine war was at its height. Their faces were black with oil, and they were singing because, incredibly, they were alive while their shipmates drifted face downwards in that terrible current, the Race, which speeds out to sea between Dinas Head and the Quies. 'Visitors are warned that bathing on the left side of the bay is dangerous at low tide.' This is where the Race springs to life. And so on another day the farmer who was fishing for bass from low rocks shouted at two heedless bathers, father and son, to warn them. The father was swept away by the current, but the boy was saved, clinging to the farmer's line. I wondered, pitiless, who would remember the clothes in a heap by the entrance to the cave before the tide came up.

Treyarnon Common linked our bay with Constantine Bay – low cliffs covered with close-cropped turf and sea pinks. The road from the farm ended at its gates, guarded by the Pinchs' cottage, which was then the only one by the bay. In the middle of the common stood a pump with solid granite trough. It was a lonely place, but once a year it was transformed by the St Merryn feast, a great annual parish celebration held about midsummer. There were wrestling matches, side-shows and a dance. A small marquee was set up and surrounded by long trestle tables and wooden benches, where several hundred people sat down on the open cliffs to a high tea of cold meats, pasties, saffron cakes, and splits and cream. Later the moon came out as the crowds strolled by the cliffs; the waves were breaking gently on the rocks below, and bats scythed the sea-scented air overhead, while the Pinchs' old white pony nosed among the remains of the baked meats on the tables. I would wonder whether I was confusing the scene with some eighteenth-century print, did not others in St Merryn still remember it.

At Constantine Bay, one birthday evening, a group of children climbed the dunes bordering the wide crescent of sand. Bare legs torn by sea holly and marram grass, slipping and sliding, eyes full of sand-stung tears, we reached the peace of a hollow where a stream flowed through a tamarisk tunnel below the ruined church of St Constantine, which was buried in sand. We made an enormous fire of driftwood, and we fried sausages. The evening primroses stood round the stream like pale yellow lights, and the rosy beam of Trevose lighthouse shone like a giant spotlight on our faces. There was a smell of bruised mint growing by the stream, mixed with the tarry smoke. Round the fire stories were told of the wrecker's cottage between us and Booby's Bay, evil of atmosphere; or of the hermit who had lived on Constantine Island and existed on shellfish, the shells being still piled in a great heap there: or of the smuggler's cottage at Constantine, from whose cellar led a passage to a cave opening to the sea. When the moon came out, our elders took little sickles with which they slashed the sand where the tide had gone down, to find sand-eels.

Northwards in Booby's Bay, on a maze of low rocks, there appeared for many years legends such as 'To the Haberdashery Department', 'Bargain Basement',

'Millinery' and 'Lifts'. Exiled from London for six months of the year, we played at shops. We sold the bleached bones of cuttlefish, strands of coral and rosy-brown cowries and frilled ribbons of seaweed. When a gentleman's dress shirt was gently deposited by the tide we painted up 'Gentleman's Evening Wear': 'sunk like a stone, trapped like a rat,' moaned our nurse, 'while he was drinking his champagne.' Between the sea and the rocks at low tide the rusting iron ribs of a great German ship, wrecked some thirty years earlier, thrust outwards in a menacing tangle. 'To the Underground' we painted on one of her plates. And what did we sell in the china department? That was easy: the broken pieces of worked flints from the midden on the lower slopes of Trevose headland. We grubbed around like terriers in the rabbit holes; scrabbling with our nails, we unearthed flakes of flint heaped there. The chippings of Cornish diamonds, painted top shells and prawns – something to treasure, something to eat – all found their way to our shop. At high tide it was submerged.

Then it was time to take the road to the lighthouse. I remember travelling it in a push-chair propelled by a dark man – my father, who was with us for the last time in Cornwall before he went to the Front and was killed at Arras. The lighthouse stood above a courtyard of houses where there were pavements which felt like London beneath our sand-shoed feet. Inside there was a dizzy spiral staircase and a powerful smell of oil. If the foghorn started, we jumped with horror at the first throaty lugubrious blast of noise. On a clear day, after the great prisms of glass which surrounded the lamp had swung round half an hour before sunset, punctually the great red light shone out every five seconds; and we watched for Godrevy's answering white light thirty miles down the coast. Waking late at night I saw the red light flash across the bedroom ceiling and slowly counted four, but sleep came again before the flash returned at the fifth second.

Where were the figures that peopled this landscape? In those days the villagers liked to turn their backs on the sea. The houses faced inland away from the south-west gales, and they left the beaches to 'furriners' like ourselves, except for their occasional outings to the bay on hot summer Sundays. Then, dressed in black, they sat on the beach far away from the sea and read the *News of the World*.

Blind Charlie drove a gig round the lanes, collecting eggs from the farms and selling them again. He wore a bowler hat and dark glasses. We thought of him every time we climbed a certain stile over a low slate wall on the high cliffs, for here it was that, while shooting rabbits, he had stumbled and shot his own eyes out. He had lain for twenty-four hours in a field below, we were told, gnawing at turnips in his pain and hunger. He lived to old age, but his end was sad. Every evening he tapped his way along from his cottage at Shop to the Farmer's Arms, until one day he fell into a roadman's trench and died of shock.

Never again in my life have I waited as eagerly as I waited for the postman, Hubert, who had a wooden leg and smelt of treacle. I stood at the garden gate looking down the hill, listening for the tap of his leg before he turned the corner. I was not waiting for a letter from any loved one, but for *Tiger Tim's Weekly* and *Little Folks*. About the day they were due I was in a frenzy of anticipation. They were my link with the outside world, showing that I was addressed and recognised as a person – not just one of a family spending the summer in Cornwall.

So many of the farming families were

Squire Old. (George Adamson)

called Old – all cousins – but the farmer at Treyarnon Farm was the only one who was known as Squire Old. His Georgian farmhouse had style; one sensed a superiority in the cluster of buildings. The fig tree at its gates, the pebbled carriage-drive, the coach-house over whose doors were fixed the painted motto and carvings from the prow of some long-wrecked boat: all made a civilised group in the rough-hewn landscape. Squire Old had a fabled walled garden. Only a few hundred yards from the sea, in the shelter of great slate walls, grew myrtles and peaches, carnations and wallflowers, lilacs and fuchsias. The smell of the box hedges in the sun mixed with the

tang of rotting seaweed and the salt airs blowing up the valley. To enter the garden on a stormy day was delicious: the cutting wind roared outside the walls, but here were calm and warmth and ease – a wonderful withdrawal from the battle that the coast fights with the Atlantic.

Leaning on his knobkerry, as if granting some aristocratic privilege, Squire Old invited us into this garden. We could see little of his face between his white straw hat and silver beard. He gave us peaches from the wall, but I was not satisfied; I had seen a honey-ripe pear, and its bell shape fascinated me. I longed to curve my hand round it – no thought of eating it. I let him lead the others out of the garden, snatched the pear and hid it in the elastic of my knicker leg. When I got home I tried to extract it unseen, but it eluded me and fell on the floor. I was castigated for my wicked theft and told to go straight back to Treyarnon Farm to return it to Squire Old.

Tears streamed down my face as I took the short cut across the fields. I arrived breathless at the farm and knocked gently. Miss Flo, the squire's sister, came to the door, smiling beneath an elaborate postiche of curled hair. 'Please give this back to the squire. I stole it.' I pushed the warm bruised fruit into her hand and fled. She called after me, 'Wait'; and soon the squire came out with a little basket of pears: 'So you are fond of pears, my dear?' In confusion I thanked him and carried them home, buoyed up by a sense of triumph; but my nurse thrust them untasted into the dustbin, murmuring about the wages of sin.

(Autumn 1966)

CAMPING WITH FATHER

Bruce Campbell

My father maintained that he spent the two most formative years of his long life as a young man in British Columbia. Turning aside from the Klondike gold rush, he began by washing bottles at a Kamloops brewery and finished, before the South African war called him away, as factotum on a remote ranch whose owner was on shooting terms with his nearest neighbour. During the long fine summers he and his friends went far afield, birdnesting, fishing or hunting, and he learned to camp rough. This experience he applied some twenty years later when we spent most of the summer of 1921 in Argyll.

Owing to the coal strike, the skies were clear over Glasgow as we travelled north, and they continued more or less blue for the next two months, giving me an idyllic but misleading idea of a West Highland summer. When the rain fell, it seemed mild and friendly; when the wind blew the surface of the sea loch into scurrying waves, it was an exciting interlude among sunny days and short glimmering nights. The season suited my father's simple technique, basic to which was the absence of a tent. On a bed of springy bracken – as immortalised in *The Road to the Isles*, which was written about that time on an island not far away – he laid an enormous army valise which accommodated him, my mother and me. Its head was stuffed with spare clothes to make a pillow; and we had blankets, raincoats and, I suppose, groundsheets over us. I cannot recall the groundsheets in 1921; they were the thin end of the orthodox wedge.

Our first night out, at the end of June, was on an island of rock and long heather where I had found my first merganser's nest. We fished for lythe in the velvety dusk, then scrambled into our bed on the top of the island. Next morning was 'soft'; I huddled under the blankets while my father started the breakfast fire among the boulders on the shore of the creek: no stoves, of course, and dry heather rather than newspaper as first ingredient. To cheer us up he sang what he said was a music-hall ditty of his youth:

All the comforts of an 'ome!
There's whiskers in the soup
And the baby's got the croup;
All the comforts of an 'ome!

I doubled up with uncontrollable laughter and forgot the midges. The weather soon cleared; and we moved camp to the next island, where we spent two more amphibious days in a mixture of paradise and the minor discomforts inherent in my father's methods.

Highland summers reverted to type after that, and school meant that I did not get north until August, when the best of the weather was usually past. We now had a cottage of our own, eight miles from the merganser's island and, though we had our fair share of holiday adventures, we seemed to end up under some sort of roof at night. But in 1927, reinforced by Freddy, a powerful young man of eighteen, my father and I decided to attempt what had been our ambition for several years – the forty-mile circuit or round-trip of Loch Shiel, both somewhat misnomers for rowing up and down this narrow fjord-like water.

We left Acharacle, the valise making a snug seat in the bows of a hired boat, at

'My father started the breakfast fire among the boulders . . .' (R. Grimshaw)

about eleven on a late August morning which seemed to promise days of fine weather. Within half an hour we had landed a 4½-lb sea trout on the troll – good omen indeed – and we slowly fished our way along the low banks of the great mosses that cushion the western end of the loch, lunching at Dalilea, where Charles Edward Stuart stayed the night. The lock narrows after that, past Eilean Fhianain, the green isle of burials, then widens between the great bare hills of Moidart and Ardgour to run, with no road and scarcely a track on either side, almost straight to its head at Glenfinnan. Our first camp was about half-way up, in a bay on the Argyll side facing the Black Rocks, where common gulls nest

and learn to wait for fishermen's crumbs.

My father led us to build a leaf shelter on British Columbian lines. I suppose its prototypes had a framework of fir poles and were filled in with flat branches of aromatic needles. This could be achieved today on our site at some damage to the Forestry Commission, because the land has been part of Glenhurich Forest for many years; but in 1927 we had only the small alders along the burns, several of which ran into our bay from the steep hillside. Fortunately alders grow straight and have reasonably spreading branches with large round leaves. We cut poles, pointed them and drove them in to make the corners of a seven-foot square; four more laid along the tops completed the main structure. This was guyed where necessary with string, which played a vital role in the construction, binding the joints and providing a loose network on two sides into which we worked the leafy branches; in British Columbia I expect they used creepers. Another concession was the roof of two groundsheets, with a third as windbreak behind our heads. The cracks in the walls were stuffed with bracken, which we also cut for bedding. Down went the valise and our arrangements were practically complete. We could lie in comfort with a view of the loch on the two open sides and gaze at what my diary called 'a real picture postcard evening, yellow sunshine, purple hills and reddy mauve water'.

This unreally beautiful atmosphere prevailed in the morning, as my father and I fished round the rocks before breakfast, prepared by the reluctant Freddy on a stone hearth near the shore. We were away by eight and were making a leisurely approach to Glenfinnan when the west wind, blowing behind us up the funnel of the loch, freshened unpleasantly. The peaty pool on the Argyll side of the Callop proved a trap, and it took us about an hour to extricate ourselves and tie up at the pier in the river where the daily steamer from Acharacle, the Clanranald, had just arrived. We gave the purser the best of our six trout to take back to my mother, made a few purchases at the tiny shop and began our return journey at two-thirty. The waves blew froth on to the beach by the Jacobite Monument as we struggled broadside over to Glenfinnan House, hoping for some protection on the Inverness-shire shore. After an hour's rest and fortifying tea we tried again. My father and Freddy took the oars but, my diary records, 'we nearly capsized as they rowed too near the bows, so we re-organised'. In fact, we tried

'My father and Freddy took the oars . . .'

(R. Grimshaw)

various combinations, even landing me to slither through the heather and bracken while the others kept close in, still looking for some lee under the rocky headlands. Eventually Freddy and I took spells at the bow oar, and we slowly passed the wide mouth of bleak Glenaladale. The rain began and, expecting the wind to drop, we landed for supper in the scrub woods below the rocks of Poll an Daimh.

At ten o'clock we were opposite our previous camp, at the delta of the Gaskan burn where there was a wood of planted trees – larch, fir and beech. Freddy caused some excitement when the tip of the rod bent as he wound in his line; in the darkness he had reeled his minnow right up to the top joint and was playing it like a fish. We stumbled across the stony burn near its mouth, spread the groundsheets over the branches of a small beech and laid the valise under it. While Freddy and I fell asleep exhausted, my father lit a wood fire – the worse the conditions, the more he was on his mettle in this respect – before going under the blankets. As he lay on his back, wondering no doubt how he was going to get us home, he saw a bright point overhead: a star, he thought, so it had cleared up after all. Then the star fell into his eye – a raindrop caught in the firelight.

'Woke up in rain,' says my diary, 'to find a supposed tree stump was Freddy's head.' After letting us lie while he explored the possibility of breaking into two empty cottages, my father organised the building of a big leaf hut with growing trees as posts. One corner was protected by groundsheets as before, and beech, with its flat branches of hard shiny leaves, was even better than alder for the sides. This time we had three walls and the open front faced the fireplace; beyond it, on a low bank, we put up a system of poles on which our sodden blankets could dry. They also reflected the heat of the fire into the hut, so that we were able to warm up in luxury, intellectually sustained by a copy of *The Bulletin* bought the day before in Glenfinnan. The scores in the final matches of the English cricket season seemed as remote as if we really were in British Columbia.

The storm continued with only minor abatements and next morning found my father 'doing Atlas to the roof, rain dripping in everywhere'. We were running out of food and faced the alternatives of going before the wind back to Glenaladale, where there was a farm, or crossing the loch at a favourable moment to the solitary croft of Gortanvorran. We had just decided on retreat when the wind dropped, so we took our chance and crossed instead. The Kennedys at the croft provided huge scones which we ate on the shore, attended by a belated young common gull whose parent warned it off when it became too confiding. At last, in the evening, the wind began to ease and we set off on our last leg. Darkness overtook us as we reached the mosses, and we spent some time gently grounded on a sandbank until Freddy pointed out that we were not moving in relation to the distant lights of Acharacle. Neil Cameron from the Lochshiel Hotel drove us home at midnight, and my mother got up to cook buttered eggs which I can still taste.

Next year, perhaps because he was fifty or realised that the summers in Argyll would never be like those of British Columbia, my father bought a tent and our camping became conventional. But, twenty-five years later, when he was an old man and my sons were staying with him, he built them a leaf hut on the edge of the woods behind the cottage. It was smaller but far more solid and elaborate than those we made by Loch Shiel, with a ram's skull to decorate the doorway. When I visited it in the winter it had already withstood the autumn's gales and seemed symbolic of all human artefacts which, once spare and useful, become ornamented and innocuous; what it had meant to my father I could only guess, but to me, standing among the bare trees and dead bracken, it was inexpressibly moving.

(Autumn 1963)

JUST FOR A LARK

R. H. Wilson

The shepherd had finished pitching his hurdles round our daily fold, and we were walking across to admit the four hundred hungry sheep, when a lark flew up at our feet. We fetched three more hurdles and set them up in a triangle to protect the nest. I visited it every day for a fortnight, until the young birds had safely flown, leaving a green oasis in an expanse of bare brown field.

Sixty years ago, when my three brothers and I were children and a spell of killing winter weather set in, we would lay a row of chaff, corn and small seeds as long as a cricket pitch on the frozen snow and ice, sited to give a good field of fire from the barn door. There we would hide and wait for the starving birds to assemble: greenfinch, yellowhammer, goldfinch, bullfinch, linnet, wagtail and every kind of tit. The gunner, lying on the floor with an antique muzzle-loader, would 'let the little bastards have it'. A flash and a violent boom, and we would rush out through the cloud of black smoke, grab about fifty dead and curse another fifty that were just able to scramble for cover. We would carry the bag up to the nursery to gloat over the corpses until

(Dudley Hoys)

they had to be thrown away. At that time the first thing to meet the eye on entering a house of any pretensions was a case of stuffed birds: corncrake, green and spotted woodpeckers, kingfisher and all kinds of finches.

What can account for the complete change of attitude towards bird life in the intervening years? My father at least had the excuse of necessity when in 1875, at the age of eleven, he arrived with sixpence in his pocket to work on his bachelor uncles' farm near Faringdon in Berkshire. They were also dealers, sending cattle and sheep weekly to Smithfield Market. The home was ruled by his aunt, whom I remember as the harshest, least sympathetic creature on earth. As a welcome, when my father showed her his sixpence, she hissed: 'And you won't have another till ye 've earned it.' Defiantly he told her not to worry, he would have £1000 when he was twenty; and he went to bed to think up some scheme to achieve it.

Next morning he jumped up on a wagon in the yard, and there saw plovers, two or three pheasants and a bunch of skylarks destined, the wagoner told him, for Leadenhall Market, where skylarks were considered a special luxury and sometimes made 4d. each. Before the week was out my father had borrowed a muzzle-loader with powder and shot from his uncles, who were always kind to him; and he was able to hand over a bunch of larks at the weekend. Some time later the wagoner, who had become his business adviser and agent, asked him how much money he had put by. When my father told him, he said: 'That's enough for a porker. Go and buy one, get it scalded and ready for me on Monday morning.' Thirty years later, in 1905, my father's dealing business had an annual turnover of £125,000.

On clear frosty nights, when I was not much bigger than a sparrow myself, I would be carried on the shoulders of a 6ft neighbour round the thatched cottages in the village and, with the aid of an evil-smelling oil bicycle-lamp, would spot the sleeping sparrows tucked in holes in the thatch, grab them with one hand and pass them down to be thrown violently on the ground.

Bird 'dubbing' was a more mature and robust 'sport'. A hurricane lantern would be placed in the bottom of a thick hawthorn hedge, and here would gather most of the party with buckets of stones. The beaters would tap the hedge along towards the lantern, flushing all the blackbirds and thrushes and sometimes a fieldfare. These would follow the hedge as far as the lantern, then flop down and be stoned to death.

'I want you boys to shoot twenty-four blackbirds,' my father once said as he was leaving home for the night, 'so that your mother can have a pie ready for my supper tomorrow.' This was just the sort of job we relished and, with the help of two schoolfellows and any sort of borrowed firearm from a four-ten to a converted army rifle, we proudly returned home with ninety-six blackbirds – enough for four pies of the traditional size. Today my brother Ted gets up from his chair twenty-four times a day to feed a pair of blackbirds which tap on his window; and the pair eat far more cheese during a week than his housekeeper and himself together.

The lowest form of senseless slaughter in which we used to indulge was 'starling flighting'. We were in the direct line of Knighton Bushes, a favourite roosting place; and just before dusk, as the birds passed over in countless thousands, we would blaze away at them, bringing down eight or ten at a time. We took not the slightest interest in the 'runners', with the result that the village was crawling with maimed starlings. The only rebuke we received came from the vicar, who once asked us to desist as he could walk scarcely a yard in his garden without stepping on a dying starling. We thought his complaint most unreasonable.

When my three elder brothers had gone back to school, I had full access to our first gun, a four-ten. Our nanny, who was the kindest person in the world, used to buy a box of twenty-five cartridges on the understanding that I killed one bird a day for her pet owl. The victim was frequently a robin, as I found him rather more daft than a cock sparrow and easier prey. I was only five years old when I shot my first rabbit; and I had killed my first flying bird, a jackdaw, before I was six.

I cannot remember how or why our blood-lust began to wane. Certainly it was not due to parental persuasion, nor to any appeal for a different attitude made in our village school. Indeed our last school-master – we have had schoolma'ms for a quarter of a century or more – was the worst nest-robber I ever came across. We boys did not discuss the subject among ourselves; yet, by the time we had graduated from bird-slaughter to bird-nesting, we pursued this hobby as a real study and with due regard for the care and protection of nests and eggs.

Before his death in 1927, my brother Jack had become a fully self-taught ornithologist who could 'see' a bird's nest through a brick wall. Once when, at the request of the South Kensington Natural History Museum, he met a party of eminent ornithologists at Swindon station, he was horrified to see that the five dear old bespectacled gentlemen had little boxes with cotton-wool. Not until they had jettisoned the lot would he take them the ten-mile drive by horse and trap to see five nightingales' nests in less than an hour.

(Spring 1969)

A POT OF TEA FOR TWO . . .

Theresa Grace

We lived in the heart of the Hampshire countryside tucked away in a downland village, in the early 1920s. Very few cars were about in those days – only the gentry could afford them and, of course, our local doctor – so anyone could walk, and we children play, in the roadway, just stepping aside if we heard anything approaching.

One day, my mother was very sad and worried, for Dad had returned from work with news that his job was finished. He was getting on in years and there was not much scope for other employment where we lived. However, Alice, my elder sister, said, 'Don't worry, Mother. We'll think of something.' And then, 'I know what we'll do. Let's serve teas.' We all laughed and thought that would be fun, but whoever is likely to pass *this* way? Alice wouldn't be daunted and found a big piece of cardboard and printed TEAS boldly on it and hung it in the front window.

'We must get out the daintiest cups and

saucers and plates, and a pretty cloth, and lay the table,' Mother said, laughing as if it was a huge joke. When Dad came in he wanted to know, 'What on earth's going on?' We told him about Alice's wonderful idea. 'Never heard such a lot of nonsense,' he began, when a knock at the door silenced him. We all held our breath. 'You answer it Alice,' Mother said. A strange voice said, 'You've saved my life. A cup of tea, please. There's nowhere open for miles.' This happened less than half an hour from the card being put in the window. A wonderful beginning and what excitement!

From that day our little cottage was seldom without someone calling in. The Cyclists' Touring Club found it and put us in their books. We often got crowded out, so my brother helped to build a large summer-house and in fine weather it was full up too. Cakes, jams and everything possible were made by Mother. We opened a visitors' book and eventually it had hundreds of entries: people even wrote little verses in praise of Mother's home-made jams and cakes. They loved our homely little tea-shop. We began to serve lunches and 'any-time' meals as well, and then Mother was asked if she could put someone up for the night. Next thing, I was being turned out of my bedroom and had to make do with the box-room.

We made so many friends who came again and again. One young lad came as a Boy Scout, regularly walking miles from the coast, where he lived. He came later when courting his girl-friend, then when she was his wife and, later still, with his children. They talked of so many happy memories of our cottage and how Mother's little tea-shop had progressed over the years. Another regular was a commercial

'My brother helped to build a large summer-house and in fine weather it was full up too . . .' (Arnold Wiles)

traveller who always arrived for lunch. We treated him like a gentleman, the table being daintily laid especially for him. He always had high praise for Mother's thinly-sliced beetroot, which was grown in our own garden. Dad did many things like that to keep up our reputation; he was a first-class gardener.

Another sister and I (we were the two youngest of a large family; the others mostly had grown up and gone their separate ways) did a lot of table waiting, always in clean, starched pinafores. We collected so many tips that we saved enough to buy our first bicycles. What joy we had and what work Mother did. She was up all hours. She brought large hams and cooked them on the range, in big iron pots. The meat was not only for the tea-shop but was also for selling in the village, for 2s. 6d. a half pound, I remember. Her charges were always low, for she hated to over-charge, and yet she made enough to save for a rainy day and to help us children on our ways too.

Later on, troops came to camp nearby, hundreds of them, on manoeuvres. They came to us for breakfast and every meal, it seemed, even at midnight, when the military police came off duty and Mother used to have an ovenful of big dishes of shepherd's pie waiting. For a good supper, often consisting of eggs and bacon, Mother charged 2s. 6d. Her teas for two, which included home-made jam and cakes, cost only 1s. 6d.

We were five or six miles from Hambledon race-course and when the big meetings were held we were crowded out but, unfortunately, not always with desirable customers. We found one man stuffing Mother's silver knives and forks down his wellingtons. Each race-day people queued all down the road while we made urns of tea.

My dear mother, she loved it all, but *how* she worked. And thanks to dear Alice and her piece of cardboard, she enjoyed so many friendships over the years.

(Summer 1984)

GRANDAD WAS A GUISER

Ernest Paulson

I never knew that Grandad had been a guiser until one night, when I was talking about mumming plays with Mother, she suddenly declaimed:

'Come, Jack, and take a drink out of my bottle
And let it flow gently down thy throttle.'

Grandad had been the Doctor and they'd played the local farms and big houses. Grandad had been a strict 'blue ribbon' – a teetotaller – so it didn't matter that there had been no pub in the little place where they lived or that they couldn't play the pub in the village up the road; that would have been poaching because that village had its own guisers. Some of the others had grumbled a bit but never on Christmas Eve, because then they always went to the big farm at the top of the Bent where there was always a barrel of good ale and plenty of good grub.

When I'd worked it all out, I realised that

Grandad must have been performing nearly a hundred years ago, but to Mother it was as yesterday. The guisers were ordinary railwaymen and labourers with blackened faces, tattered and fantasticated clothes and straw wigs; they spoke and sang in high, assumed voices and went round with the mumming play or singing, dancing and telling stories. In the ordinary way they wouldn't have dared to act as they did, but a blackened face and a drop or two of seasonal lubrication worked wonders.

In Grandad's troupe, he – the herbalist – was the Doctor, the Jester was a platelayer who lived next door and kept saddleback pigs on his allotment, the Turkish Knight was a long, spidery shunter with arms like an ape. 'Dad had to watch him like a hawk when he fought St. George, else he'd win.' St. George – 'the noble champion bold' – was a ponderous engine-driver from Up-Plantin'. The Jester never let his children have a pig's bladder to play football with; every one went away in the store-shed either for his Christmas performance or for his missus to fill with lard at pig-killing. He was a small, wiry man, a good dancer and a powerful tenor, but he'd never sing at church concerts because he and the Rector didn't get on. Instead he always sang for the village over the hill where he could be sure of a free pint or two.

They'd meet on Christmas Eve, drifting casually through the darkness – there wasn't more than one gas-lamp in the place – to the chapel room near the sidings. The railway signal-lamp was a good guide. There, by the light of a candle lantern, they'd black-up in the swinging shadows, puffing vigorously at their pipes to kill the stink of mould, mud, rotting hay and cats; for the chapel had been an old barn which the Primitive Methodists had converted by using upstairs for the chapel and leaving the downstairs to look after itself. When they were all ready, they'd troop out into the muddy lane and make their inconspicuous way to Barn Lane and the big farm.

They'd cross the big pasture to the stile where they'd stop to light the lantern; and as soon as they did so, there was always a yell, for all the kids from the farm cottages would be there, waiting. Then the whole lot of them would scuttle off, screaming 'They're coming!' to reassure the farmer, who knew he'd be first but always worried that somebody else would supplant him.

At the farm, all was ready for the visitors. Milking had been done early, every man and animal had been fed and a special batch of baking done. The big table was loaded with pies, cakes and a big ham, a barrel of the best beer was under the window and another table near it was loaded with pots and glasses. A big brass lamp over the table lit up everything. The guisers, awed by all the magnificence, gathered round the door and gaped at the shining steel grate, the brilliant black range, the winking copper pans on the wall, the loaded gun and the hams hanging from the beams, the big dresser with its serried blue-ware – and then concentrated on the ham and the barrel under the window.

'Come along in,' bellowed the farmer, and his wife, daughters and sons and the farm men and maids smiled invitingly. In they went. Farmer ran his eye over them. 'Where's . . .?' he began, then stopped. He wasn't supposed to know who they were. The platelayer grinned, then struck up a song to cover the gaffe.

After the play had been played, the fun began. Attempts to discover identities were resisted till everyone broke down in laughter, stories were told, songs sung, everyone ate and drank hugely and flirted shamelessly until the farmer's wife called them to order and it was time to go. Farmer would slip a florin into the Jester's ready

'The stile where they'd stop to light the lantern . . .' (Brian Walker)

hand and the farewell carol would mingle with the sound of the bells ringing for the late night service. Away down the lane they'd go, the chant of 'We *wish* you a merry Christmas' getting fainter until the door closed.

Back at the chapel, they'd clean off the black at the water-butt, agree to divvy up after they'd been round on Boxing Day and then, splitting into ones and twos, make their way home to bed. Tomorrow might be Christmas Day, but the hens and pigs would need feeding just the same.

When they stopped, Mother didn't know. Grandad had died quite young, around the turn of the century. All I remember is that as a small boy I was once blacked-up to go with a party to get some cash for our missionary boxes. The leader got a hiding for begging and the rest of us were told to go home and behave ourselves. That was in the Twenties.

(Winter 1983)

----------------------------- TAIL CORN -----------------------------

Gloucestershire woman, warning neighbour against some brightly coloured apples: 'They looks a'right, but when yer gets yer teeth in 'em they're that teart as to put yer ears back two inches.'   *(Autumn 1955)*

[153]

The countryside near Wroxton, Oxfordshire. (John Saunders)

THE PAST AROUND US

GUNPOWDER VALLEY

Rebecca Thatcher

Hot and out of breath, I struggled to the top of the hill, to the ancient chapel of St. Martha astride the Pilgrims' Way. I sank down on the seat by the south wall and gazed at the valley of the little river Tillingbourne below, which lies between the hill and the village of Chilworth a few miles south of Guildford in Surrey. It was a peaceful scene: horses and cows grazed in the lush grass, a farmer was loading manure on to a trailer and people were walking along the footpath which leads from the village, past the seventeenth-century manor house to the chapel. Through the valley the river wound its way into the distance.

But it was not always so tranquil. It was busy enough to make William Cobbett, riding by in 1882, fulminate: 'This valley, which . . . seems formed for a scene of innocence and happiness, has been . . . so perverted as to make it instrumental in affecting two of the most damnable purposes; in carrying into execution two of the most damnable inventions that ever sprang from the minds of men under the influence of the devil! namely, the making of *gunpowder* and of *bank-notes*!'

Of the two, Cobbett much preferred gunpowder which could, he pointed out, be 'meritoriously employed' against tyrants. To make it, required water power and charcoal, both of which the wooded valley of the Tillingbourne supplied. We may still trace the industry's archaeology here.

One of the basic ingredients of gunpowder is saltpetre, the chief source of which was the droppings from doves and pigeons. A process for purifying saltpetre was perfected at the beginning of the seventeenth century, and in 1625 the East India Company set up gunpowder mills 'on the edge of Windsor Forest'. At this time the forest stretched well into Surrey and it is believed that these early mills were at Chilworth. In 1636, the appointment of powdermaker to the King was given to Samuel Cordwell and George Collins of the Chilworth mills and they became the only authorised gunpowder-makers in the country. £2,000 was loaned to them by the Crown to extend the factory and an order was sent to mayors and other local officers, instructing them to assist Cordwell and Collins in acquiring carts and barges to transport the powder to London.

About this time Aubrey wrote, 'In this little vale are sixteen powder mills. They now belong to Morgan Randyll of Chilworth manor, one of the representatives in Parliament of the town of Guildford.' By 1677, when Sir Polycarpus Wharton took over the mills, they had become so run-down that he spent £1,500 of his own money to put them in working order. It did him little good, for he lost a fortune on the venture as the Crown would not pay its bills, and he ended up in a debtors' prison. Still, powder-making continued there for more than two hundred years. In 1885 the Chilworth Gunpowder Company was formed, the factory was rebuilt and extended until it

ABOVE: *Trees grow up among the ruins of First World War powder mills along the banks of the Tillingbourne.* (Bob Collins)

RIGHT: *Skeleton of a water-wheel.* (Bob Collins)

stretched for two miles along the valley. Then tragically, in 1901, an explosion in the Black Corning House killed six men and injured many others.

The Black Corning House was a two-storey building, the lower storey being below ground level and under the bank of the river. Here, powder cakes, made in a separate building, were crushed and granulated by means of two water-driven mills. From the Corning House three men were taking powder in barrels on a tramway to the Dust House some fifty yards away. The ground was frozen hard and the men wore nailed boots. It was thought that the cause of the explosion could have been a spark from one of their boots igniting the powder on the trolley.

The damaged buildings were repaired and in the First World War the factory worked twenty-four hours a day. After the war, the demand for gunpowder diminished; all the manufacturers amalgamated into Nobel's Explosives, later to become part of the chemical giant ICI, and in 1922 the site was sold. It is now owned by Guildford Borough Council and is preserved as an open space.

I left the chapel and followed the footpath down to the valley passing Chilworth manor, now the home of Sir Lionel and Lady Heald. Lady Heald told me that the manor was built on the site of an eleventh-century monastery and pointed out a stew pond in the garden which was a source of fish for the monks. The manor saw the building and the disappearance of the gunpowder factory and remained unchanged by either. The only change was brought about by Sarah, Duchess of Marlborough, who lived at the manor in the early part of the eighteenth century and who added the north wing and a walled garden. From the manor I walked along the bank of the river, bluebells stretched in a haze for as far as I could see.

I came upon a row of millstones, half buried and overgrown. A little further along

Millstones that once ground the king's gunpowder, now overgrown and abandoned. (Bob Collins)

[157]

several brick pillars and a heap of twisted metal, then, almost covered by ivy, a ruined building. Across the river was part of a narrow railway – the route the powder had taken on its way to Chilworth Station. Still further along the bank, almost at the eastern end of the site, a whole row of derelict buildings. Enough of them remained to see that they had been of two storeys, the lower below ground level: the powder mills built after the explosion.

The whole site was littered with bricks and tangled metal, but nature had incorporated them into its plan and gradually they are disappearing under a carpet of nettles, brambles and ivy. The trees that had been cut down to provide charcoal have grown up again. It is almost as if 'that damnable invention' had never existed. If he were here today, I'm sure William Cobbett would be well pleased.

(Summer 1982)

Powder mill debris is washed away into the river. (Bob Collins)

GRANDMA'S LAMP ROOM

Donald Hodge

I never smell paraffin without recalling a tiny room just inside the back door of the house where my grandmother lived in a Kentish village. Long before the advent of gas or electricity, the weekly visit of the oilman was one of the fixed events. His horse-drawn cart carried a stock of candles (tallow and wax), matches and black-lead, lamp glasses and wicks, but the chief item was the big tank of paraffin. There was a smaller container of colza oil as well, but the demand was mainly for paraffin. From the houses he would collect the domestic cans, fill them from the tap on the tank, and light and heat were guaranteed for another week.

In Grandma's lamp room the routine never varied. Every morning the lamps were collected and taken to the lamp room. There were the big ones from the parlour and the living room and the smaller ones from kitchen and passage – it was candlesticks and candles in the bedrooms. There were hand lamps too, as well as the hurricane lamp for outdoors.

First of all, off came the glass chimneys for cleaning and polishing. Then it was the turn of the reflectors. These were usually of tin, concave and plain or fluted, though one lovely lamp had a mirror glass reflector. Then the reservoirs had to be filled using funnel and oilcan, and the wicks trimmed. And woe betide anyone who left a 'horn' on a wick, for when it was lit there would be a smoke mark at least and a cracked chimney quite possible. Then

(Brian Walker)

came the final wipe with the cloth before each lamp was restored to its proper station.

Day after day, year after year, the routine was the same. Even in summer there was the odd one or two to be done, for the windows were so tiny that parts of the house were never really light. So it was small wonder that there was a dew of paraffin from floor to ceiling in that little room. It could never be eliminated, and the chief aim was to confine it to the lamp room.

Few commodities are as insiduously pervasive as paraffin. Once I climbed the tower of Dungeness lighthouse when the illuminant was still paraffin, and on every surface – stairs, walls and balusters – there was a patina of paraffin oil. And for me, whenever that odour strikes my nostrils, immediately, I am whisked away, across time and space, to Grandma's lamp room.

(Autumn 1979)

THE LITTLE LAUNDRY MAIDS

Amoret and Christopher Scott

When we acquired our sixteenth-century half-timbered cottage in Worcestershire, our predecessors showed us the foundations of a large building in the paddock behind the house, and a small leather-covered book which had been passed on to them by the previous owners. The site had been occupied by a laundry which was run as a training school for young girls from local institutions. The book had been used by the matron of the establishment, who lived with her staff in our cottage, to record the advent, progress and subsequent fate of each of her charges. Their average age on arrival was about twelve, though in 1888, one, Edith Crane, was admitted at the age of seven. All had originally been taken into institutions with a background of broken homes: dead, crippled, insane or worthless parents. A common formula is 'Father dead, mother deserted her'.

From 1870 until 1925, when the home was finally closed, there is a complete record of the running of the laundry. The girls washed all the linen of the great house which patronised it, and neighbouring houses could have their washing done at reasonable prices. In 1905 damask tablecloths up to three yards long were laundered for 6d.; nightdresses cost 8d., 9d. or 1s. 6d., depending on whether they were white, flannel or silk.

There seems no doubt that the establishment was well and efficiently run according to the somewhat stringent principles of the time and circumstances. It was inspected annually, and there were regular visits by the chairmen of the unions from which the girls came. While the reports inscribed in the book are uniformly complimentary, one cannot avoid the picture of the pathetic twelve-year-olds who lived and worked there, pummelling the huge sheets and tablecloths in an atmosphere of steam for most of the hours of daylight (and a good many dark ones in winter) and packed off to bed in the long bare dormitories. In some of their reports the inspectors do remark that the girls seemed to be working over-long hours. Their pleasures were obviously few. Country dancing was allowed once a week; those who could sing at all attended choir practice, and all were scrubbed for church, where attendance was compulsory three times on Sunday.

If the girls had a thin time of it, the matron's patience must often have been sorely tried. 'Five girls were so rude to Mrs Kitching that they were punished by having no pocket-money and no eggs for breakfast. They object to doing their work over again when not properly done.' 'Florence Ratcliffe's character not very satisfactory. She cannot get up in the morning.' 'Mary has to remain out of the laundry, she is so naughty.' One particularly unfortunate affair involved Trumper, the boiler man and only male in the establishment, Mrs Kitching the laundry matron and Ethel Anderson, one of the girls.

> '25th July, 1893: Trumper has been very troublesome this week in putting the girls up to mischief and sauciness. He is also a great deal too familiar with them, especially Ethel Anderson.
>
> '28th July: Matron has had a serious talk with Ethel. She had, however, been very impudent to Mrs Kitching and was sent to bed in consequence.
>
> '4th August: Trumper has been given notice to leave, chiefly on account of the girls'.

It must be added, however, that the rebellious Ethel went on to make good and was finally placed as housemaid in an unknown mansion, whence favourable reports were received.

Not all of the girls survived the rigours of the laundry, and even the first laundry matron, in 1871, became 'mentally affected'; eventually she drowned herself. Several girls are recorded as being untrainable and were returned to the institutions

from which they came. One complete page of the book contains a name, date of arrival and the laconic statement, 'Ran away'.

When they had made their own 'trousseaux', an essential part of which were two pairs of black knitted stockings, most of the girls were placed in the great houses of England at wages ranging, in the 1870s, from £12 a year for a fifth laundry maid to £14 for a second, plus 2s. 6d. a week beer money. Those not sturdy enough to do laundry work were found other forms of domestic employment at reduced rates: in 1874 Caroline Hall was sent out as an under-kitchenmaid at the wage of £7 a year – and no beer money.

The home must have been a blessing to

ORDNANCE SURVEY

Crossed swords on the map – site of
   battle,
This bee-buzzing meadow of green,
Ruled now by a boy and his cattle,
Where once such confusion had been.

What slashing, what piercing and
   smiting!
What trampling, what dealing of death!
What groaning, what fiercely delighting!
What looting before the last breath!

How tiny this field, for the making
Of dynasties born in a day.
How still now this valley where, aching,
Survivors came, limping, away.

Long gone, the proud battle flags
   blowing,
All perished, the panoplied gains.
The victors long dead, never knowing
That nothing they fought for remains.
Hugh Russell (Summer 1982)

the governors of local institutions, which were always overflowing with the debris of unhappy households. Although the girls had a hard life they did at least reap the benefit of decent occupations in an age when unemployment was the rule rather than the exception. The foundations of the laundry will probably remain in the paddock for all time, for they go deep into the soil.

(Winter 1960)

TO AN UNKNOWN SHEPHERD
AND HIS WIFE

The marsh lies empty where their
    cottage stood –
Their names have no importance – only
    the tears
Of the woman when they found him,
    and the good
Heart of the shepherd cross the
    unknown years;
Four hundred years of lambing-time to
    shearing,
Bad times with good, repeated grief and
    joy,
And muddled human will, strong
    beyond fearing,
That meets the moment's need, though
    it destroy;

All this, the pity and the pride of life,
Shines from the tale of a forgotten pain
    –
The stubborn shepherd and impatient
    wife
Greet us like kinsfolk through that
    distant rain,

Not as great heroes, not as martyrs,
    these, but such
As for the little of their simple lives,
    gave much.

S. C. Boorman
(Spring 1978)

On the mountain track from Talybont to Anglers' Retreat, Cardigan. (Bridget Beresford Horsley)

ONCE A DALESMAN

Alan Walbank

On a blue and white February day this year, when there was a keen north wind and a glistening snow-cap on Whernside, but warm sunshine in the shelter of limestone walls, I walked the six-mile length of the green road known as Mastiles Lane. It runs from Malham at the source of the Aire to Kilnsey in Wharfedale. I was in the company of a hundred and fifty young people, all making protest against a proposal to macadam for motor traffic this old turf way. Nobody who walked it, whether motorist or not, wanted the road to be turned into another gritty or oily black ribbon. We prefer to share it with sheep, curlew and, in season, scatterings of the yellow mountain pansy. I especially, having taken this road my first day out on my very first schoolboy journey of exploration, hoped that another generation would be anxious to keep it green.

In the ten years before the 1939–45 war the green roads of the Yorkshire dales were the links in my regular spring, summer and winter walking tours, binding together all the most desirable inns, farms and villages of overnight stay without need to set foot on metalled surface. I lived in a small industrial town, went to school in a city, but for a few days of each holiday trod only turf. Weeks beforehand it was part of the exciting prospect to plan a round, taking in fresh daleheads, hamlets, 'scars' and 'forces' – rocky outcrops and waterfalls – and to push out the exploration by a day or two's march, always observing the same rule.

So the links extended from Mastiles Lane to Horsehead Pass, to the Stake, the Gallops, the Shawl, old Cam High Road (a Roman street) and Shaking Moss, Stockdale Lane and Flock Rake: all green roads except where farm tracks, but not tractors then, had followed them occasionally. By this means, enjoying a solitude and silence broken only by the grace notes of wind or running water, I soon joined to Wharfedale the neighbouring Coverdale, Wensleydale, Cotterdale, Bishopdale, Dentdale, Garsdale, Barbondale, Ribblesdale, Kingsdale, together with the nearer Littondale and Langstrothdale. Where these drovers' ways 'ow'r t' tops' ended there were riverside paths, or sometimes narrow flagged causeways with V-shaped stiles, to follow through the meadows. On the upland stretches a tree and a spring together were carefully noted on days of high summer for the midday halt: in the fields boots whitened not with dust but with pollen. When pressure of time and explorer's enthusiasm drove me hard to cover the ground between perhaps three valleys in the day, I learned to relish the dews of both morning and evening.

These early explorations, in days before the Youth Hostels Association and Pennine Way, fostered self-reliance, indifference to desolate places and rough weather, and keen appreciation of simple joys – bathing in silk-smooth peaty pools, treading bare-foot for a whole day on springy turf, seeing cotton-grass cover moorland like a shimmering blanket, watching a skein of geese or a nest of weasels at play. Contact with the dalesfolk rubbed in a wry humour, reserves of independence and a new sense of life's realities.

When two of us, knapsacked khaki-shirted boys of sixteen, turned up at dusk in

Middlesmoor in Nidderdale. (Alec Wright)

a Nidderdale village and looked for bed and breakfast at a cottage, the first question was 'Are ye out o' work?' And when the man of the house, who was, began somewhat half-heartedly to help his wife with preparations for a meal, his effort was checked by: 'Oh, don't you put your body in an uproar, I'll do it myself.' The meal of lardy cakes and onion scones was to us as exotic as it was economical. Then came the question of tea: 'Do you fancy a cup or a pot?' Thirst demanded a pot; but we were not quite prepared for the large pint-size blue-flowered vessel filled for each of us with a black steaming brew from a brass tap beside the fire oven. Next morning, after an uneasy night spent in dodging the depression of an old double feather bed, and breakfast of thick-cut salty bacon and

drip-bread, we paid our three shillings and were bidden to come again, any time.

Hospitality in this exciting region beyond the mills and millstone grit was what one might call latitudinarian. In one dalehead farm at which I arrived in a downpour at day's end I seemed to be the only guest. So, after supper and a thorough drying out before the huge fire, I sought an early bed. About midnight, as it seemed, I slowly became conscious of a red glow in the bedroom and odd noises of splashing and whispering from behind the washstand. Fire, I thought; where's the door? The glow persisted, but there was no heat and it grew no ruddier; the whispering died down. Eventually sleep claimed me until daybreak. It was only then I found the cause. Two cyclists had come to occupy the room's other bed, screened off by a curtain: they had been developing some exposed film by the aid of a rear-light. Nobody had thought to mention their presence. This, of course, was a generation before the tourist trade justified its place as the Yorkshire dales' second industry, after agriculture.

At another farm in the high dales, mention of supper brought a blank look to the housewife's flushed face. They were too 'throng' with the hay. Then an idea came: we boys could have it with them free, if we would help first. It was not quite eight o'clock and we agreed. So with rakes and rolled-up sleeves we went down through several fields to the lower pasture. Turning hay began, with all the farmer's family out. Dusk fell, twilight deepened; we did not seem like stopping. Then the moon came up, the hay gleamed silver and all continued with renewed speed. The moon rose high above the valley; we were still working for our supper and earning it. Only when the distant church clock had struck one was a halt called. Then we trooped wearily back to the farm to sit down round a long table scrubbed lily-white and lit by a pink-globed oil-lamp.

The real bonus came the following day. Looking round for some lunch at the next small town, we saw a market 'ordinary' and went in. Our farmer of the previous night spotted us and tipped the waitress a wink. So we paid our shillings and received bigger helpings of beef, vegetables and Yorkshire pudding than even schoolboys on a walking tour could manage, followed by freshly baked apple pie and a large wedge of creamy Wensleydale cheese.

Two impressions left by this kind of exploration were lasting and formative. First there was a sense of the inexhaustible freshness and wonder of the natural world. As morning mist cleared, dew twinkled topaz and emerald on the turf, and we caught our first glimpse of Semerwater in remote Raydale; with a hovering hawk the only creature in sight, it might have been the very beginning of civilisation. Such pastoral parts of the country showed scarcely a sign of modernity. All was green or grey, sparkling, unchanged – fell, sky, water, stone. Hay came down from the high pastures on wooden sledges, not tractors; there were no weekend motor-boats on the lake; caravans never mottled the meadows. Added to this was consciousness of the slow march of change and the permanence here of old styles and simpler ways.

Industry had advanced no farther and left no more signs than the flue system and conical chimney, or the octagonal chapel-like form of lead smelting mills such as those in Apedale and Arkengarthdale, built about 1700 and long disused. Many of the farms and barns had stone panels with seventeenth-century dates. Inside their living-rooms and in daily use there might be a court cupboard, carved and initialled in dark oak of the same period. Water came from spring or village pump. In one hamlet, Horsehouse in Coverdale – the dale from which came Miles Coverdale, translator of the Bible – it was said to flow by the way of the graveyard; but no one seemed the worse. At the shoeing-smith's all the sheep marks for miles around were branded on the wooden half-door so that farmers could identify any stray. A local squire whom I met once walking in the ditch near Redmire said he always used the grass verge or ditch because he could not abide this 'new-fangled macadam'. For him the old lead miners' routes across the fells and the corpse road on Kisdon Hill were modern enough.

The freedom of the dales meant a sturdier view of life. It brought the chal-

Ruins of smelting mill in Arkengarthdale. (Alec Wright)

lenge of new frontiers: Stainmore Forest, the Tees, Cauldron Snout, with the dramatic surprise of England's highest inn at Tan Hill and such hamlets as Whaw, Booze and Punchard on the way. The turn of every hill and river had its excitement. With it came the content of unchanging ways, cultivation of the long view and of the pace that would last, sure knowledge that every fell had its smooth as well as rugged side.

As I revisited those quiet places to which green roads lead, I found more interests being pursued and more discoveries to make than in many a city. For an expert bibliophile, a botanist, archaeologist, alpine florist, collector of Wesleyana and of feldspar, I need look no farther than to two villages. A silversmith and a watercolourist and a porcelain enthusiast are almost neighbours. If indeed the demands of work and war had not plotted otherwise, I might have done like the artist who went from the city to paint Castle Bolton thirty years ago and, having become once a dalesman, still finds it too difficult to decide when to go back.

(Autumn 1965)

DARTMOOR PEAT

B. Crocker

In our village of South Zeal and nearby Sticklepath, both in the parish of South Tawton, wood for burning is scarce.

Until the coalman arrived with his lorry about a quarter of a century ago, we relied for heat on the peat, or dags, which we cut every year on Dartmoor in the third and last weeks of September. As a social event peat cutting came next in importance to the club walk and agricultural show; all but the very aged took part.

Early in the morning men, women and children left the village in carts and wagons loaned by employers and supporters for the occasion. On board was plenty of refreshment, including good farm cider, the gift of the transport owners. When they arrived at a spot selected many months earlier, the men staked out their claims, while the women settled down to knit, sew, gossip and keep an eye on their young. Cutting continued until midday. Then came a break, and all ate their fill of pasties, bread, cheese, ham, pickles and other substantial fare. The peats were stacked with plenty of air-space between the layers and later transported back to the village, where each man built his rick, thatching it with ferns or straw; thus the supply of winter fuel was assured.

The peat fires were never let out; they were banked at night, and burned up merry and bright when the ashes were raked out next morning. At the Warren House Inn, between Moretonhampstead and Princetown, there is a fire that has been burning for two hundred years, though not in the same hearth. Some years ago the old inn was in bad repair, and another was built across the road. The fire was kept going until this was ready for occupation; then the smouldering turves were transferred to the new hearth, where the fire still burns.

(Autumn 1962)

MY SIEGE IN THE TITHE WAR

Doreen Wallace

Some youngish local asks me, 'Wot's that-air grut memorial on the hill above Wortham chu'ch? Din't moy granpa tell me that were toime you had them Blagshutts on yar farm?'

I feel sad. Did his grandpa tell him nothing but the Blackshirts? Nothing about the rural strife, 1932–1939, northwards from Kent where it started to south Yorkshire, through East Anglia and the Midlands and westwards to Cornwall? The Tithe War?

Well, here is the truth about them Blagshutts. I was there, at Wortham, southwest of Diss and just in Suffolk. I was the wife, am now the widow, of the farmer concerned, who had been county-courted for arrears of tithe and whose pig-yards were distrained upon and guarded night and day by court bailiffs.

We got busy on making it difficult for any lorries to collect 134 fat pigs. The yards adjoined a public road, but for some time the council had been asking us to dig a ditch to keep flood-water from the yards from running on to the road, so we set our farm-hands to dig a ditch six feet deep and six feet wide. The only other approach to the yards without trespass was by a farm-track, gated midway, with a fine tree standing on each side of the gate. We sold the trees to a timber merchant who employed a highly-skilled feller to cut them down; this man said afterwards, tongue-in-cheek, 'Can't think how that happen: Oi

Novelist Doreen Wallace and her farmer husband Rowland Rash outside their Suffolk farm in 1934, carrying effigies of General Dealers and Queen Anne, which were later burnt in protest after the forced sale of twenty-nine of Rash's cattle for non-payment of tithe. (Associated Press)

never done that afore. Criss-crawss they fall, blockin' the geat. No cart can't git through till they're gawn.'

So how were General Dealers (the Church's company set up on a capital of £2) to remove 134 pigs? It took them six weeks and a dummy run to think out a plan. It resulted in a sort of sedan-chair for one pig at a time, manhandled from one side of the ditch to the other, and it took hours.

During those six weeks, the Blackshirts occurred. One dark evening a man came to the back door and asked leave for 'his lads' to camp in a field. When he had told us who

they were – a small band of London East-Enders in black shirts – we told him they might camp but we would have no communication with them, the Tithe-payers' Association being totally non-political; and they must do nothing to interfere with the course of the law (we had already done enough, all legal and above-board).

And nothing is what they did. They were terrified if an old cow coughed in the night, and sent a messenger down to the house gasping 'They're coming, they're coming,' to be sent back by our house-garrison with a flea in his ear. And the lot of them, about

20, we thought, were swept up by the police to appear at the Old Bailey before the 'siege' came to an end.

So that is the Blackshirt story, and how sad that it is the only thing remembered of our long war against tithes.

It was the declaration of World War Two that put an end to active resistance: farmers had their patriotic duty to do. But before then a good deal happened in the Tithe War. The 1936 Act reduced the amount payable by 14 per cent but had a sting in its tail – it made tithe a personal debt, which gave the Church the opportunity to make me bankrupt in June 1939. I was the only one rich enough to risk testing the law – being then a successful writer – so, since I had recently become chairman of the Tithe-payers' Association, I faced up to my duty, cleared all my cash out of my bank and told my publisher not to pay me anything pro tem, and forced thereby the sale of all my household goods in a marquee on the lawn – an event very widely publicised by the association. It was a lovely party – crowds of tithe-payers from near and far. The former chairman at once bid the required sum on the association's behalf, the sale stopped, the furniture went back into the house – the whole operation being reported by every newspaper and the *Pathé News*, including the subsequent revels round a bonfire: marvellous publicity.

Then came the Nazi war; after which, as after World War One, a great deal of land changed hands, and by the 1936 Act either the seller or the buyer had to redeem the tithe, so the number of persons interested in resistance became fewer and fewer, and now there is no more tithe. But why, oh why, is the local memory of the many distraints confined solely to the arrival, at one scene, of 'them-thar Blagshutts'?

(Winter 1984)

LOOK LEFT FOR BADGERS

H. F. Ellis

The other day, in one of those monumental clearances that the tidy-minded non-hoarder never enjoys, I threw away two old road maps. The larger, covering southern England with London and environs on back, could just about be unfurled to its full extent by an angler with ape-like arms accustomed to indicating the size of the salmon that got away; the other must have been more wieldy in its heyday but had become so curiously creased and torn that the back, delineating northern England, kept coming (if I make myself clear) to the front, so that a flap with Preston on it would very likely intrude upon some quiet county like Dorset. The great new arterial roads and by-passes were shown, in the approved fashion, in blue; and it was then I noticed that the most impressive of these were the Kingston By-pass and the Great West Road, that sections of Western Avenue remained to be constructed, and that the Exeter By-pass was still only a dream, or a nightmare, that I decided that the maps could now be dispensed with.

The interesting thing about both was their narrow-minded devotion to the task of guiding the motorist from A to B. It seems to have been thought in those days – the 1930s, I suppose – that all he required was the names of towns and the roads connecting them. It is a fact that the 'explanatory symbols' on the larger map were confined to 'Bridge over Railway' and 'Railway Bridge over Road' (one would have thought that the average motorist, even then, was capable of recognising the nature of these obstructions when he came to them), plus a little flag indicating 'Principal Racecourses', which can have got in only through some quirk or predisposition on the part of the publisher. Not a cathedral nor a castle interrupted the tranquil 6ft journey from Ramsgate to Penzance. No woods nor viewpoints. You would look in vain for windmills or Silbury Hill. Go racing or get on was the watchword of the times.

We have come a long way since then. The modern motorist feels rightly disgruntled if a glance at his road map fails to tell him, by means of green shading, whether the scenery he is passing is worth looking at or not. At my next clear-out I shall throw away all maps that have no symbols for barrows, airports and botanical gardens. Wordsworth must have had the road map of the 1960s in mind when he wrote:

Ships, towers, domes, theatres, and
    temples lie
Open unto the fields, and to the sky;

and he could have added, given some looser metrical arrangement, parish churches, pylons, wireless masts, recommended inns, steep hills, birthplaces of famous men, worthwhile detours, caravan sites with water laid on, and all-night garages. He could have gone further. I have before me a quantity of advertising matter on behalf of both the *Reader's Digest/AA Book of the Road* and the *Sunday*

Times/RAC Road Atlas, though I have not yet (having earlier been given the *Reader's Digest Complete Atlas of the British Isles*, so that I already know the distribution of latter-day saints and bream in East Anglia) actually ordered either of these tremendous works. It is clear from the publicity that each of them marks a considerable step forward. The AA maps have a symbol for parachuting and another for Highland games, both new to me, and the RAC indicates 'Sandy Beach' with a clarity never approached since the forgotten days of wind-blowing cherubs and 'Here be sandy beach'. An incredible quantity of additional information is available on, alongside, before, behind, above and below the maps themselves, so that the motorist need never be at a loss to identify a roundabout or a tithe barn, a clouded yellow or a bit of milky quartz, stratocumulus or a differential, nor fail to realise in advance that Acton Round (Salop) is a quiet village with interesting church.

There are those, I dare say, who will be satisfied with either the AA publication, which has 'the best road maps of Britain on the market', or the RAC one, of which I read that, 'This new road atlas provides the best and most complete answer so far to motoring map-reading, route-finding and planning.' I shall not. These maps may be good, but they are clearly not complete. There is still too much hunting about to be done in the back pages. The busy motorist who wants to miss nothing *en route* – not a folly nor a blewit, not a convenient coffee stop nor a view over undulating park-like country (1 mile on left) – cannot be expected to turn to page 189 in order to learn that the area he is passing through has the greatest density of sheep south of a line Wash to Bristol Channel. He wants the whole thing at a glance. He may learn (RAC map) that Great Dixter is a place of interest, because it is printed in red, or that he is approaching (AA) an archaeological monument (symbol like a pawnbroker's sign, in blue); but what is the use of that if what he wants at the moment is a recommended cup of tea? He has still to have recourse to the *AA Handbook* or, for fuller information, the *AA Guide to Hotels and Restaurants* (or whatever may be the RAC equivalents); and even then he cannot be certain that the AA's recommendation has not in fact been condemned outright by 'Bon Viveur' for flabby lettuce. I reckon that, for a full informed journey, the alert motorist will still need some fourteen auxillary maps and guides at his elbow, including the Ordnance Survey map of Roman Britain in case he should miss Viroconium altogether.

How long we shall have to wait for the complete road map, I do not know. It must give as much prominence to snack-bars as to windmills. It must cater for all the varied interests of motorists. Not all of us confine our enthusiasm to abbeys and youth hostels; there are philatelists, too, and others who would be glad to know that they were approaching an antique shop specialising in Victorian brass beds. Some ingenuity will be needed to compile a series of symbols designed to convey their meaning at a glance; we shall be back where we started if we have to hunt through forty-eight pages of explanatory matter to find out what the green pyramid with red asterisks shooting out of its apex down the

next side-turning but two can possibly foretell. I would suggest, for instance, that a brown cup surmounted by a triangle outlined in some combination of colours, with the figure '12' over-printed on the cup, could stand for a pleasant wayside inn serving coffee up to noon and sandwiches recommended by Egon Ronay and the AA, but not mentioned in the *Good Food Guide*. There ought to be some easily recognisable way of colouring, emarginating or otherwise distinguishing stretches of the A2 in order to warn nature-lovers that it is a waste of time to look out for Dartford warblers in the area. It is not my responsibility to set down in detail exactly how the thing should be done. Possibly the chosen section of road map can be made to unroll itself at a speed equivalent to that of the car, with perforations along the edges producing a continuous stream of information through a loud-speaker attachment (optional extra), so that any car journey would be at least as informative as a trip down the Thames from Westminster Pier.

When this new complete road map is ready, or perhaps before that, I think I shall rummage about in the dustbin to see whether my old 1930 maps have survived. They may be out-of-date, inaccurate and only held together here and there by bits of sticky paper, but they do give a driver a chance of concentrating on the matter in hand.

(Winter 1968)

──TAIL CORN──

Irishman watching a friend sifting through a box of bits and pieces: 'You never know. Something may come in handy one day, even if you never use it!'   *(Summer 1977)*

Somerset farmer: 'Oi've zeventy-foive chicks going cheap.' Friend: 'What do ee expect 'em to do – bark?'   *(Spring 1972)*

INDEX

Note: page numbers for illustrations are given in italics.